9.95

107 QUESTIONS CHILDREN
ASK ABOUT PRAYER

107 Questions Children Ask about Prayer

General Editor:
Daryl J. Lucas

Contributors:
David R. Veerman, M.Div.
James C. Galvin, Ed.D.
James C. Wilhoit, Ph.D.
Richard Osborne
Jonathan Farrar

Illustrator:
Lil Crump

Tyndale House Publishers, Inc. Wheaton, Illinois

Library of Congress Cataloging-in-Publication Data

107 questions children ask about prayer / general editor, Daryl J.
Lucas ; contributors, David R. Veerman . . . [et al.] ; illustrator, Lil
Crump.
    p. cm.
    ISBN 0-8423-4542-6 (pbk.)
    1. Prayer—Christianity—Study and teaching.   2. Christian education
of children.   3. Prayer—Christianity—Miscellanea.   4. Children's
questions and answers.   I. Lucas, Daryl.   II. Veerman, David.
BV214.A13   1998
248.3′083′4—dc21   92-23034

Printed in United States of America

04	03	02	01	00	99	98
7	6	5	4	3	2	1

CONTENTS

INTRODUCTION

WHAT PRAYER IS

What is prayer? **1**

What is prayer for? **2**

Why do we have to pray instead of just asking God? **3**

Why do we have to pray to God? **4**

Why is it good to pray? **5**

Why do people pray to idols? **6**

Who do we pray to—God or Jesus? **7**

Why did Jesus pray? **8**

When we're bad, can we still pray? **9**

Who is not allowed to pray? **10**

*Why do we have to pray when God already knows what we
are going to pray?* **11**

If God is invisible, how can we know he is around us? **12**

How can God be everywhere? **13**

How does God feel when we pray? **14**

HOW TO PRAY

How do we pray? **15**

*How does God know what we're saying if we're praying in
our head?* **16**

Is it OK if we pray really fast or slow? **17**

Does how we pray matter? **18**

Why do pastors pray long prayers? **19**

Why do people pray on their knees? **20**

Do we have to fold our hands to pray? **21**

Should we make the sign of the cross when we pray? **22**

Why do we shut our eyes when we pray? **23**

What is a prayer closet? **24**

Can't we pray anywhere? **25**

Do we have to pray certain prayers? **26**

Why did Jesus say we should pray the Lord's Prayer? **27**

Is it bad to memorize a prayer and say it every time we pray? **28**

Does God listen to any prayer, big or small? **29**

Why do people say "thee" and "thou" when they pray? **30**

Why do we say "amen" when we're done praying? **31**

WHEN TO PRAY

Why do we call it "saying grace"? **32**

What is the difference between food that we pray for and food that we have not prayed for? **33**

Why do we have to thank God at every meal when he already knows we're thankful? **34**

Do we still have to thank God if we don't like the food? **35**

Why do we pray before we go to bed? **36**

Why do we have to pray when we don't want to? **37**

Why do we have to give thanks for things we don't like? **38**

Why should we go to God for help? **39**

Why do people wait until the last minute to pray? **40**

What happens if we don't pray at all? **41**

What happens if we're interrupted when we're praying? **42**

What does "praying continually" mean? **43**

Does praying a lot make a person better? **44**

Can we pray anytime we want? **45**

WHAT TO PRAY FOR

What do we need to pray for? **46**

Are there some things that we shouldn't pray about? **47**

Can we tell God everything we want to? **48**

Does God want us to pray for our friends? **49**

Can we pray for animals? **50**

Do we have to pray for people we haven't met before? **51**

Can we pray for money? **52**

Can we ask God to give us things like toys? **53**

Is it OK to pray to get something that our friends have? **54**

Is it bad to ask God for something we don't really need? **55**

If we prayed to find something we lost, would we really find it? **56**

What if kids are mean to us and it's hard for us to pray for them? **57**

Why do we pray for our enemies? **58**

Can we ask God to help us pass a test? **59**

When we're sad, can we pray that someone will come play with us? **60**

Why do we pray to God to help us not be bad? **61**

Why do we ask Jesus into our heart? **62**

Do we have to pray to be forgiven? **63**

Can God help us pray? **64**

ANSWERS TO PRAYERS

How can God hear our prayers from heaven? **65**

If we talk to God, does he always hear us? **66**

How does God concentrate on millions of people all praying at once? **67**

Does God usually give us what we pray for? **68**

Does God only give us things that we need? **69**

Why doesn't God give us some things we pray for? **70**

How do we know God is answering our prayer? **71**

Why doesn't God answer prayers right away? **72**

If we're discouraged and it seems like God doesn't answer our prayers, what should we do? **73**

When we pray for someone not to die and then they die, does that mean that God didn't love them? **74**

If God has it all planned, can we really change it by praying for things? **75**

Why does God not answer our prayers the way we want? **76**

If we pray for something one night, do we have to pray for it the next night? **77**

How come God answers some people's prayers and not others'? **78**

Why do some people write down when God answers their prayer? **79**

How does God answer our prayers? **80**

When God says we can pray about anything, does he really mean anything? **81**

Does it matter how much faith we have? **82**

PRAYING FOR OTHERS

How do we know who to pray for? **83**

How does praying help sick people feel better? **84**

How come missionaries need so much prayer? **85**

What do prayer warriors do? **86**

PRAYING TOGETHER

What should a person do who feels embarrassed to pray in public? **87**

If we don't like what someone prayed for, what should we do? **88**

Why does God want us to pray together? **89**

Do children have to pray with an adult? **90**

Is group prayer more powerful? **91**

Why do some people hold hands while they're praying? **92**

BEDTIME PRAYERS

Do we have to pray every night? **93**

What if God has already answered all of our prayers? **94**

If we've prayed all through the day, do we still need to pray at night? **95**

Are your daytime prayers as effective as your night ones? **96**

After our parents pray with us, do we still need to pray on our own later? **97**

Why are we sometimes forced to pray? Shouldn't we pray when we want to? **98**

How can we think of something good to pray about if we've had a bad day? **99**

Do we have to pray even if we're tired? **100**

Is it bad to fall asleep when we are praying to God? **101**

ON A WING AND A PRAYER

How come some people are asking for sunshine while other people are asking for rain? **102**

Can we pray for snow so we can't go to school? **103**

Does God only answer serious questions? **104**

Is it OK to complain to God? **105**

Doesn't God ever get tired of answering prayers? **106**

What is the Lord's Prayer? **107**

INTRODUCTION

"Dear God, thank you for the world. Thank you for my new Mega Torx Jeep. And please make it so it doesn't rain tomorrow so I can go to the pool. In Jesus' name. Amen."

A heroic effort for a six-year-old at dinnertime? An adequate prayer? As much as you can expect? Pitiful?

Prayer does not come naturally to children any more than riding a bike does. Children come into the world needing a relationship with God, not with the relationship already working. Like new adult Christians, children need to be introduced to God and coached on how to talk to him. They need to find out what prayer is, why they should do it, and how it fits into their walk with God. They need to learn how prayer works. Then they need to learn *how* to do it. Although at some point most children *will* pray, their prayer will be weak, underpowered prayer if they have never been taught the principles God has so graciously given. But what a wonderful, adventurous relationship with God awaits those who *have* been taught! To teach a child to pray is one of our greatest responsibilities.

Of course, *teaching* children to pray does not come naturally either. Where do you begin? What do you say? How do you answer the tough questions?

Those questions are the reason for this book. We collected hundreds of questions children asked about prayer, then identified 107 of the most common and important ones and sorted them into categories. If you are a parent of children ages three to ten, or if you work with children, you have surely heard questions like them. If not, you soon will.

We identified Bible passages relevant to each question and then summarized the Bible's application to that question. Study the Scriptures listed with the questions, because the Bible has a lot to say about prayer. It doesn't answer every question directly, but it gives principles that Christians should know and live by.

As you answer children's questions, keep in mind the following points:

- "Silly" questions are serious questions. Always take a child's questions seriously. Do not laugh at them. Some questions may sound silly to you, but they are not silly to your child. Be careful not to ridicule your child's ideas or mistaken notions.
- Some questions reflect a child's immediate personal concerns. When a child asks, "How can we think of something good to pray about if we've had a bad day?" (question 99), he has probably had a bad day *that* day. Instead of just answering the question, take time to ask about his day. Or if she asks, "Do children have to pray with an adult?" (question 90), she has probably suddenly realized that she can pray by herself, and she is asking for permission to do so. Give your permission enthusiastically instead of just saying yes. Assure her that *she* can pray *all by herself* and that God would love it. "In fact," you might say, "if you wanted to pray by yourself while you were walking to school, you could just start talking to him. That would be great!"
- The best answers come from Scripture. The Bible does not answer every curious question we have, but it does have many principles and guidelines for how we should pray. We need to be informed about them so that our prayer habits conform to God's design. After all, God invented prayer, and he did it for our own benefit. It only makes sense to study his instruction book! Study the Scriptures listed with each answer, including the Related Verses, for God's timeless wisdom.

- The best answers avoid theological jargon. Use normal words. Children think in terms of their own experience, so abstract concepts have no meaning to them. As much as possible, talk about *things, events,* and *objects* they are familiar with. Talk about activities they can imagine doing. Give them something to look at in their mind. If they can imagine it, they will understand it.
- Some questions have no answer. Be careful not to make up an answer when you do not have one and when the Bible is silent. If you do not have an answer, say so. Or suggest that you look for the answer together. If you invent answers, your child will eventually lump the Bible with other childhood stories and fables. Emphasize the truths and guidelines of Scripture that you *do* know. And express your trust that God does have answers and will reveal them in his own time.
- Some kids just want to keep asking. Be ready for follow-up questions, and be willing to keep talking. Your answer may lead to more questions. That is the mark of a good answer—it makes the child think.

We wrote this book to help you answer kids' questions about prayer. We sincerely hope and pray it does that.

—Dave Veerman, Jim Galvin, Jim Wilhoit, Daryl Lucas, Rick Osborne, Jon Farrar, Lil Crump

WHAT PRAYER IS

Q: WHAT IS PRAYER?

A: Prayer is the way we talk with God, just as conversation is the way we talk with our friends and parents. It is the way God has given us to thank him and to ask him to be involved in our lives.

Prayer is an important part of a friendship with God. Friends talk with each other a lot. It is the same with God and his friends. God's friends talk to him. They communicate. They pray.

KEY VERSE: *O God, listen to my prayer. Pay attention to my plea. (Psalm 54:2)*

RELATED VERSES: *Ephesians 2:18; Colossians 4:2; 1 Timothy 2:1; Revelation 8:3-4*

RELATED QUESTIONS: *Why is praying called praying? Who made prayer up?*

NOTE TO PARENTS: *Prayer is not a goal in itself. The goal is the relationship with God and all that comes with it. Help your children to understand this, and the process will be easier for them to grasp.*

Q: WHAT IS PRAYER FOR?

A: The purpose of prayer is for us to get closer to God. When we tell God that we are sorry for our sins, thank him for all he has done, and ask for his help, God begins to change us. He changes our thoughts and desires, and he shows us what he wants us to do. We come to love him more and to see things from his point of view. Also, prayer gives us an opportunity to say, "Your will be done." It is a way for us to work with God to change the world. Think about it this way: God is our Father. He loves us and wants to meet our needs, to teach us how to live, to take care of us, and to use us. He wants to be our friend. Prayer asks him to do that in our lives. We pray because it invites our loving Father to work in our lives and in our world.

KEY VERSE: *You haven't done this before. Ask, using my name, and you will receive, and you will have abundant joy. (John 16:24)*

RELATED VERSES: *Psalms 4:1; 17:6; Philippians 4:6; James 5:16; 1 Peter 3:12*

RELATED QUESTIONS: *What's prayer supposed to be for? Is praying good?*

NOTE TO PARENTS: *Prayer is a lot like a conversation between a parent and a child. This analogy will help you explain prayer.*

A: Prayer does not have to be very formal and serious. Prayer can be natural, like having a talk with a friend. Whenever we have a need, we can just talk to God. We can tell him what we are excited about, tell him what worries us, or ask him for help. So when we pray, we *are* just asking God. We are talking to our best Friend.

We can pray about anything, anytime, anywhere, because God loves us.

KEY VERSE: *I prayed to the Lord, and he answered me, freeing me from all my fears. (Psalm 34:4)*

RELATED VERSES: *Philippians 4:6; 1 Thessalonians 5:17; 1 Timothy 2:1; Philemon 1:4*

RELATED QUESTIONS: *Why is prayer so complicated? When I pray, why does my mind wander? What's the meaning of prayer?*

NOTE TO PARENTS: *Prayer should be a very normal part of a child's life. The more conversational and real-life we make it, the easier it will be for children to understand. Prayer should not be so overly formalized that it becomes detached from the rest of their lives.*

Q: WHY DO WE HAVE TO PRAY TO GOD?

A: We have to pray to God because he is the only one who can answer. He is the only one who can give us what we need. And only God can satisfy our *deepest* needs—the needs we don't even know we have. God is everywhere and knows everything and can do anything, so he can hear everyone's prayers and answer them. Praying to ancestors, idols, angels, or people does not make sense because only God can answer prayer.

Praying to God is an awesome privilege. God made it so that we could get to know him, our heavenly Father, and have him care for us, teach us, and meet our needs. It's not a bad thing that we "have to pray." It's a good thing!

KEY VERSES: *Bend down, O Lord, and hear my prayer; answer me, for I need your help. Protect me, for I am devoted to you. Save me, for I serve you and trust you. You are my God. (Psalm 86:1-2)*

RELATED VERSES: *1 Kings 8:38-39, 60; Psalms 17:6; 32:6; 66:19-20; James 5:16*

RELATED QUESTIONS: *Why do people pray to God? Why do people say prayers?*

NOTE TO PARENTS: *Although prayer is to be an important part of our disciplined daily routine, we should always present it as an awesome privilege and encourage our children to see it that way. Making them pray or being stern about it won't give them a long-term desire to pray.*

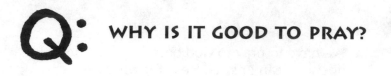

Q: WHY IS IT GOOD TO PRAY?

A: Praying is good because it brings us closer to God, our heavenly Father. Being a Christian means having a relationship with God. Prayer is a part of that relationship. Friends talk with each other, and God is our friend. Prayer makes our relationship with God better. We wouldn't have a very good relationship with him if we never talked to him.

It is also good to pray because God tells us to do it. All that God is and wants is good. Those who love God know this. They try to obey God and do what pleases him. So even though we may not always feel like praying, we should pray anyway because God says it is good to do. And if he says we should do it, then that is what is best for us and our lives.

KEY VERSES: *But you, dear friends, must continue to build your lives on the foundation of your holy faith. And continue to pray as you are directed by the Holy Spirit. Live in such a way that God's love can bless you as you wait for the eternal life that our Lord Jesus Christ in his mercy is going to give you. (Jude 1:20-21)*

RELATED VERSES: *Matthew 5:44; Luke 22:40, 46; 1 Timothy 2:1, 8*

RELATED QUESTIONS: *Why do we pray? Why do we talk to God? Why should we pray? Why do you have to pray?*

NOTE TO PARENTS: *Our relationship with God is to be the foundation of our whole life, and prayer is the communication element of that relationship. Therefore, prayer is the key to life the way God meant it to be. Our children need to realize how important prayer is. We wouldn't forget to eat, sleep, or dress every day, and prayer is more important to our lives than those things.*

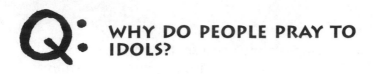

Q: WHY DO PEOPLE PRAY TO IDOLS?

A: Some people pray to idols because they believe that idols have power to change things. That is, they believe in a false god. They believe that their god hears and answers their prayers.

Other people pray to idols out of habit or superstition. They do not really know or believe in their idol. They just hope something will happen if they pray.

Praying to idols is wrong because idols are not really gods. They are just things. They are not alive and do not hear. They cannot answer prayers or bring good fortune. God wants us to place our trust in him and not in idols or superstitious beliefs.

KEY VERSES: *Yes, they knew God, but they wouldn't worship him as God or even give him thanks. And they began to think up foolish ideas of what God was like. The result was that their minds became dark and confused. Claiming to be wise, they became utter fools instead. And instead of worshiping the glorious, ever-living God, they worshiped idols made to look like mere people, or birds and animals and snakes. (Romans 1:21-23)*

RELATED VERSES: *Exodus 20:4; Psalm 17:6; Isaiah 2:8; 1 Corinthians 10:6-7, 14*

RELATED QUESTIONS: *What if we're praying to the wrong god and we don't know? How do we know we are praying to the right God? How come everyone needs to pray to God?*

NOTE TO PARENTS: *Making a wish when blowing out birthday candles, wishing on a star, or throwing coins into a well can be used as an example of why some people believe prayers to idols will bring them good luck. If your children wish at these times, let them know it's just for fun. If they really want something, encourage them to talk to God about it.*

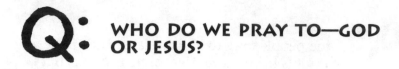

Q: WHO DO WE PRAY TO—GOD OR JESUS?

A: When a person prays, it is all right to talk with God the Father, with Jesus, or with the Holy Spirit. You can find prayers to all three in the Bible. Some prayers are addressed to God the Father, some to God the Son, and some to God the Holy Spirit. That is because God is one. We have one Lord, not three. So when we pray to God the Father, we are praying to God. And when we pray to God the Son, we are praying to God. And when we pray to God the Holy Spirit, we are praying to God. We cannot mess it up by saying the wrong name.

The important thing is that the person prays to the Lord of heaven and earth, the living God. It is what is in a person's heart that counts. Beyond our words, God sees our hearts and knows our thoughts and desires.

KEY VERSE: *Dear friends, I urge you in the name of our Lord Jesus Christ to join me in my struggle by praying to God for me. Do this because of your love for me, given to you by the Holy Spirit. (Romans 15:30)*

RELATED VERSES: *Psalms 84:8; 88:1-2; Luke 11:2; Acts 4:24; Ephesians 1:17*

RELATED QUESTIONS: *Is it bad to pray to angels? Should we pray only to God?*

NOTE TO PARENTS: *Jesus taught his disciples to talk to the Father in Jesus' name. This is a good way to guide our children because most of them can understand a father-child relationship. God wants to love them, care for them, and teach them as their heavenly Father.*

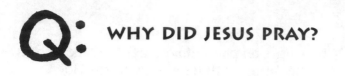

Q: WHY DID JESUS PRAY?

8

A: Jesus is the God-man. That is, he is fully God and fully man, a whole human being. Because Jesus lived on earth as a man, he had human needs. It made sense for him to pray just as it makes sense for us to pray. He depended on his Father for all his needs. He also loved his Father and enjoyed being with him, so he wanted to spend time talking with him.

Jesus was also perfect. He did everything that God wanted. God told his people to pray, so Jesus obeyed his Father and prayed.

In other words, Jesus prayed for the same reasons we do—he needed God, he loved God, and he wanted to please God.

KEY VERSE: *While Jesus was here on earth, he offered prayers and pleadings, with a loud cry and tears, to the one who could deliver him out of death. And God heard his prayers because of his reverence for God. (Hebrews 5:7)*

RELATED VERSES: *Matthew 19:13; Luke 5:16; 6:12; John 17:20; Romans 8:34*

RELATED QUESTIONS: *Does Jesus pray? Does God pray?*

NOTE TO PARENTS: *God doesn't stand on the sidelines and judge our every move. He is our loving Father. He is alongside us, helping us, teaching us, caring for us. When we fall, he is right there to help us up, strengthen us, teach us, and encourage us forward.*

Q: WHEN WE'RE BAD, CAN WE STILL PRAY?

9

A: A person can pray at any time and in any
need. When people do bad things or make
mistakes, they need God more than at any other time.
When we do something wrong, we need to talk with
God about it. We need to admit that what we did was
wrong, say that we're sorry, and ask him to forgive us.
That is the first thing we should pray when we do
something bad. Then God can help us learn so that we
can do better next time. God knows we are not perfect,
and he wants to help us by giving us wisdom and
helping us change.

If we wait until we are good enough to pray, we will
never pray.

KEY VERSES: *But the tax collector stood at a distance and
dared not even lift his eyes to heaven as he prayed.
Instead, he beat his chest in sorrow, saying, "O God, be
merciful to me, for I am a sinner." I tell you, this sinner,
not the Pharisee, returned home justified before God. For
the proud will be humbled, but the humble will be
honored. (Luke 18:13-14)*

RELATED VERSES: *Psalms 51:1-2; 66:18-19; Isaiah 1:15-20*

RELATED QUESTIONS: *Does everyone in the world pray? Are
you only allowed to pray if you're totally good? Can
animals pray? What if I injure someone? Will God still
give me what I ask?*

Q: WHO IS NOT ALLOWED TO PRAY?

10

A: No one is so bad that he or she is not allowed to pray. God is always willing to accept the person who comes and asks for forgiveness. God does not ban people from praying.

Some people have turned away from God so much that they never pray. They do not pray because they don't feel any need to pray and don't want to.

Are there any prayers that God does not welcome? Yes. God does not welcome the prayers of people who disobey him all the time and are happy about it. (They may even brag about their sins.) When these people pray, they do not really mean to have a relationship with God. Instead, they just go through the motions. Prayers from people like that are just empty words. The first *real* prayer that God wants to hear from them is *I have sinned. I was wrong. I am sorry. Please forgive me.*

KEY VERSE: *The Lord is far from the wicked, but he hears the prayers of the righteous. (Proverbs 15:29)*

RELATED VERSES: *Proverbs 28:9; Isaiah 1:15-16; Zechariah 13:9; 1 Timothy 2:8*

RELATED QUESTIONS: *How can you pray when you're a baby? Do people who aren't Christians ever pray? Does the devil pray? If you don't have God in your heart, should you ask him (for things)? Can sinners pray?*

WHY DO WE HAVE TO PRAY WHEN GOD ALREADY KNOWS WHAT WE ARE GOING TO PRAY?

11

A: When we pray, we talk to God about the things that we and God are doing together. God designed the universe to work a certain way, and prayer is part of his plan for how it works.

One of the most important reasons for praying is that it changes the person who is praying. When we pray, we become more like God wants us to be. We learn something from *God!*

Also, God wants to have a friendship with us. No one would say, "Why do we have to talk to our friends?" Talking with God just grows out of loving him and being cared for by him.

KEY VERSES: *When you pray, don't babble on and on as people of other religions do. They think their prayers are answered only by repeating their words again and again. Don't be like them, because your Father knows exactly what you need even before you ask him! (Matthew 6:7-8)*

RELATED VERSES: *Psalms 32:5-6; 139:4; Ephesians 6:18; Philippians 4:6; Colossians 4:2*

RELATED QUESTIONS: *If God knows everything, then what's the point of praying? If God knows everything we're saying and everything we're thinking, why do we have to pray at all? How does God know what we're going to say? How does God know everything? How does God know what we're thinking? Why does God know everything?*

NOTE TO PARENTS: *Help and encourage your children to say prayers that do not always involve asking for something. They can talk to God about what is going on in their lives and tell him what they are excited about. Also, encourage them to ask for needs that are intangible, such as wisdom, guidance, and help.*

Q: IF GOD IS INVISIBLE, HOW CAN WE KNOW HE IS AROUND US?

WE CAN'T SEE THE WIND, BUT WE CAN SEE WHAT IT DOES. GOD'S LIKE THAT: WE CAN'T SEE HIM, BUT WE KNOW HE'S HERE.

12

A: It is a little bit like believing in a country you have never been to. Other people have told you about it, you have read about it, and perhaps you have even met people from that land. All of this together tells you that the country is real. You yourself have never been there, but that does not stop you from believing it exists. You have plenty of good reasons to believe that it does.

Although we cannot see God, we know by faith that he is around us. That is, we accept that God is there because the Bible says so, because we have met God's people, and because it makes sense to us. So by faith we believe and trust that he is there even though he is invisible.

KEY VERSE: *From the time the world was created, people have seen the earth and sky and all that God made. They can clearly see his invisible qualities—his eternal power and divine nature. So they have no excuse whatsoever for not knowing God. (Romans 1:20)*

RELATED VERSES: *Psalms 23:4; 139:7-12; John 3:7-8*

RELATED QUESTIONS: *When you're praying, how can you feel God? Why is God invisible? Sometimes it's kind of hard to pray to an invisible person. If I can't see God, how can he see me? How come you can't see God? Is God invisible? Why is God invisible?*

NOTE TO PARENTS: *When your children ask why they can't see God, make sure you explain that God is invisible because he does not have a body like ours, not because he is trying to hide from us. As we get to know him better, we begin to see how he works on our behalf and how he shows his love.*

Q: HOW CAN GOD BE EVERYWHERE?

SCRATCH
SCRATCH

BIBLE

13

A: God is spirit, not just a big person. That is, God is not limited to space and time. He has no body that can only be here or there.

Also, God is *all-powerful,* not just very powerful. That is, he can do anything. He can be all places at once just by wanting to.

We human beings have physical bodies; we can be in only one place at a time. But God is not like that. He is always there to love us, to help us, and to listen to our prayers. And he wants us to know this so we will never be afraid to come to him.

KEY VERSE: *But who can really build him a worthy home? Not even the highest heavens can contain him! So who am I to consider building a Temple for him, except as a place to burn sacrifices to him? (2 Chronicles 2:6)*

RELATED VERSES: *Job 42:2-3; Psalms 103:22; 139:2-3, 7-8; Proverbs 15:3*

RELATED QUESTIONS: *How does God stay by everyone at once? Is God always watching us? How does God know what we're doing right now? How can God be within us all at one time? How does God go to three places at once?*

NOTE TO PARENTS: *The fact that God is everywhere and sees and knows everything should be a comfort to your children. He is always there to love, help, and listen. He does not merely spy on us or wait for us to mess up so he can punish us. Trying to make children behave by telling them that God is watching every move they make puts God in the wrong role.*

Q: HOW DOES GOD FEEL WHEN WE PRAY?

14

A: God is very happy when we pray. The Bible makes it clear that God is glad to hear from us and rejoices over us. He loves us and wants us to love him. So God is delighted when we come before him, just as a loving father is happy when his children come to him. The father welcomes his children with open arms and listens carefully to everything they say because he loves them so much.

KEY VERSE: *The Lord hates the sacrifice of the wicked, but he delights in the prayers of the upright. (Proverbs 15:8)*

RELATED VERSES: *Psalm 141:2; Isaiah 62:5; Zephaniah 3:17*

RELATED QUESTION: *Does God love the people who don't pray to Jesus?*

NOTE TO PARENTS: *This is a good opportunity to reinforce God's extravagant love for us. Take every opportunity to tell your children how much God loves and cares for them.*

HOW
TO PRAY

15

A: People pray in many different ways. All prayers don't have to be alike. So we should not worry about saying just the right words or holding our hands a certain way. God wants us to be ourselves and talk to him about the things that we are thinking about, concerned about, or excited about. We can talk to God in our very own words.

At the same time, we should realize that we are talking with the Creator and Ruler of everything. Even though God wants us to use our own words when we pray, he does not want us to be silly or to make a joke of prayer. We should be very respectful toward God.

KEY VERSES: *Pray like this: Our Father in heaven, may your name be honored. May your Kingdom come soon. May your will be done here on earth, just as it is in heaven. Give us our food for today, and forgive us our sins, just as we have forgiven those who have sinned against us. And don't let us yield to temptation, but deliver us from the evil one. (Matthew 6:9-13)*

RELATED VERSES: *Jeremiah 29:13; Luke 11:2-4; James 4:10; 1 Peter 4:7*

RELATED QUESTIONS: *What if you didn't know how to pray? Should we pray like Jesus when we pray? How should we pray to Jesus? What happens when we pray in a bad way?*

NOTE TO PARENTS: *Try not to reduce prayer to a set of how-to's. Prayer is about having a relationship with God. Any relationship a child has with God will be a little different from an adult's. Relax. God loves being with your children in all their different stages of growth, just as you do. Make prayer relevant by encouraging your children to be themselves.*

HOW DOES GOD KNOW WHAT WE'RE SAYING IF WE'RE PRAYING IN OUR HEAD?

16

A: God knows everything, even what we keep to ourselves. He knows every thought of every person on earth. He knows what is in everyone's head. Nothing that anyone thinks or feels is hidden from God.

Praying silently means focusing our thoughts on God and talking to him in our head. He hears every silent prayer.

Of course, sometimes it is better to pray aloud, such as when we are praying with another person. And praying aloud can help us concentrate when we are praying on our own. But God hears us either way, whether we say the words or just think them.

KEY VERSES: *O Lord, you have examined my heart and know everything about me. You know when I sit down or stand up. You know my every thought when far away. (Psalm 139:1-2)*

RELATED VERSES: *Psalms 94:11; 139:23-24; Matthew 6:6-8*

RELATED QUESTIONS: *People say that God just wants you to talk to him like he's your good friend. Is this true? What kind of prayer should we pray? How does God hear you when you're not talking? How do you pray without saying anything out loud? How come people pray with their mouths closed? Why do people whisper when they pray? Is it better to pray in your heart than to pray out loud?*

NOTE TO PARENTS: *From time to time your children may ask if they can pray a certain prayer silently or to themselves. Encourage them to do so. It is a good sign that they are trusting God with things close to their heart that they may feel embarrassed to say even to you.*

Q: IS IT OK IF WE PRAY REALLY FAST OR SLOW?

THANK YOU GOD, AMEN.

17

A: The speed of a prayer is not important. What matters is that we pray in a thoughtful manner. Sometimes we pray fast because we are excited. That is fine. But people who pray *very* fast may just be repeating a memorized prayer or saying certain words out of habit and trying to finish quickly. Whenever we pray, God is listening right then, and he does not want us to just speed through some words that we always say.

Sometimes we pray slowly because we are being thoughtful about what we want to say to God. But sometimes we pray slowly because we are letting our thoughts wander. It is always best to keep our attention on God.

Fast, medium, or slow, prayer should be a real talk with our heavenly Father.

KEY VERSES: *As you enter the house of God, keep your ears open and your mouth shut! Don't be a fool who doesn't realize that mindless offerings to God are evil. And don't make rash promises to God, for he is in heaven, and you are only here on earth. So let your words be few. (Ecclesiastes 5:1-2)*

RELATED VERSES: *1 Kings 8:54-55; Ecclesiastes 5:3, 7; Matthew 6:7; Hebrews 10:22*

RELATED QUESTIONS: *How does someone pray in sign language? Does it make a difference if you pray silently or aloud? Do you have to pray slowly so God can hear you?*

NOTE TO PARENTS: *Before praying with your children, help them think of a few things they are concerned or excited about, and encourage them to talk to God about these things. This will help make each day's prayers sincere and relevant and not just something to get done.*

Q: DOES HOW WE PRAY MATTER?

18

A:

Yes. We should pray *sincerely, secretly,* and *respectfully.* To pray sincerely means to pray in plain words that say just what we mean to say. It means we do not try to use fake language or fancy words. We tell God whatever is on our mind in the words that we would normally use, because he loves us and knows us and wants to care for us.

To pray secretly means to make a habit of praying alone. (Some people call it quiet time.) It means we take time out of every day to talk to God all by ourselves. We do not limit our prayers to church, meals, or bedtime with Mom or Dad.

To pray respectfully means to treat God as God. It means we do not make light of prayer or act silly. We are talking to God, the Maker of all creation, the Lord of the universe, and the King of kings, so we show him honor and respect.

KEY VERSE: *The sacrifice you want is a broken spirit. A broken and repentant heart, O God, you will not despise. (Psalm 51:17)*

RELATED VERSES: *Proverbs 1:7; 28:9; Matthew 6:5-13; Hebrews 10:22*

RELATED QUESTIONS: *Why do some people pray in different languages? How come people pray when they're talking out loud? How come people mouth words when they pray? Do people whisper prayers because they're embarrassed?*

NOTE TO PARENTS: *If we get wrapped up in exactly how our kids must behave, position themselves, or talk when praying, they may get the idea that God expects a performance instead of a sincere expression. Give your children room to grow in the exact way they pray.*

Q: WHY DO PASTORS PRAY LONG PRAYERS?

19

A:

Pastors pray long prayers because they have a lot to pray about. They are responsible for caring for a lot of people and want to pray for the concerns those people have.

Also, a lot of people ask pastors to pray for them. Many churches have a "pastor's prayer" as part of the worship service. At that time the pastor prays aloud for the needs of the people. At the same time, the people in the congregation should also pray, silently, for each need that the pastor mentions.

Keep in mind that God listens to kids just as much as to pastors. If you pray, God hears and answers your prayers the same as he does for the pastor.

KEY VERSES: *So we have continued praying for you ever since we first heard about you. We ask God to give you a complete understanding of what he wants to do in your lives, and we ask him to make you wise with spiritual wisdom. Then the way you live will always honor and please the Lord, and you will continually do good, kind things for others. All the while, you will learn to know God better and better. (Colossians 1:9-10)*

RELATED VERSES: *1 Chronicles 21:16; Acts 2:42; 6:2-4; 1 Thessalonians 1:2; 5:17; 1 Timothy 2:1-4*

RELATED QUESTIONS: *Why do some people pray very long prayers? Sometimes I want to stop praying. Should I? Is there a limit to your praying? How many words do you have to pray? Why do our pastors pray?*

NOTE TO PARENTS: *God hears and answers your child's prayers as much as he does a pastor's. Be careful not to give your children the idea that their prayers are not as effective as those of "important" people.*

Q: WHY DO PEOPLE PRAY ON THEIR KNEES?

humble   happy   tired

20

A: The Bible tells of people praying in all sorts of positions. Some stood and raised their hands. Some lay down on the ground. Some put their head between their knees. Some sat down. Some kneeled. Some stood but bowed their head and beat on their chest. We can pray in almost any position.

Some people kneel in prayer to show respect for God. It is their way of saying that they want to do things God's way. Kneeling makes them feel humble and submissive to God, which is the right attitude to have in prayer.

KEY VERSES: *He walked away, about a stone's throw, and knelt down and prayed, "Father, if you are willing, please take this cup of suffering away from me. Yet I want your will, not mine." (Luke 22:41-42)*

RELATED VERSES: *1 Kings 8:54; 2 Chronicles 6:13; Acts 20:36; James 4:10*

RELATED QUESTIONS: *Why do you kneel down or bow your head when you pray? Do you have to be in a certain position when you pray? Is it more respectful to get on your knees when you pray? Is getting on your knees a symbol of humbling yourself? Why do people pray sitting down? Why do people pray lying down? Why do we go on our knees or sit down when we pray? Is it better to pray on your knees? What is the difference between praying when you're standing or sitting?*

Q: DO WE HAVE TO FOLD OUR HANDS TO PRAY?

21

A: No. Our hands can be in any position when we pray. It is not the position of our hands that God loves but the attitude of our heart.

But most people fold their hands for a good reason. Some fold their hands to show respect and that they are bringing a request. Sometimes people fold their hands to keep them from doing anything else that might distract them from focusing on their prayer. So folding hands during prayer can be a good idea, but God does not require it. In the Bible, God's people often raised their hands to pray, as some people do today.

KEY VERSE: *So wherever you assemble, I want men to pray with holy hands lifted up to God, free from anger and controversy. (1 Timothy 2:8)*

RELATED VERSES: *Psalms 28:2; 37:7; 46:10; 141:2*

RELATED QUESTIONS: *Does it make any difference whether you fold your hands or put your hands over your head when you pray? Do you have to have your eyes closed and hands folded to pray? Why do people bow their heads when they pray? Why do most people fold their hands when they pray? Does it matter if we don't fold our hands? Why do some people stare when we raise both hands above our heads or fold our hands?*

NOTE TO PARENTS: *It is not that a particular position for your hands or body must be followed, but once a position is chosen, a reminder to stay in that position until the "amen" can really help concentration.*

22

A: Some people make the sign of the cross when they pray to show that their prayer is in "Jesus' name" (because Jesus died on the cross). It is a bit like folding hands or kneeling—God does not require it of us, but some people do it to help them pray. It reminds them that God hears their prayers because Jesus died for them.

Always remember that God cares more about our being honest and sincere than about the exact way we sit, stand, kneel, or move when we pray.

KEY VERSE: *We do this by keeping our eyes on Jesus, on whom our faith depends from start to finish. He was willing to die a shameful death on the cross because of the joy he knew would be his afterward. Now he is seated in the place of highest honor beside God's throne in heaven. (Hebrews 12:2)*

RELATED VERSE: *Galatians 6:14*

RELATED QUESTION: *Does God care how you pray as long as you're praying?*

NOTE TO PARENTS: *If you teach your children certain traditions in prayer, take the time to explain what they mean and why you feel they are important. Helping your children understand a tradition will help them get more out of it.*

Q: WHY DO WE SHUT OUR EYES WHEN WE PRAY?

23

A: We shut our eyes mainly to help us concentrate on our prayers. Whenever our eyes are open, we can see everything going on around us, and then we think about those things. We don't think so much about God or about talking to him. So people close their eyes when they pray because it helps them concentrate on what they are saying.

We can pray with our eyes open. Eyes open or shut doesn't matter to God. It's just that we need help concentrating, and closing our eyes helps us do that.

KEY VERSE: *But the tax collector stood at a distance and dared not even lift his eyes to heaven as he prayed. Instead, he beat his chest in sorrow, saying, "O God, be merciful to me, for I am a sinner." (Luke 18:13)*

RELATED VERSES: *Psalm 123:1-2; John 17:1*

RELATED QUESTIONS: *Why does my dad make me shut my eyes when I pray and then when I tell him it doesn't say in the Bible we have to, I get sent to my room? Is it best to pray when you're closing your eyes? Does it really matter whether our eyes are open or shut when we pray? Why do your parents and teachers make you close your eyes when you pray? What difference does it make if I close my eyes when I pray, or not?*

NOTE TO PARENTS: *Some young children have trouble keeping their eyes closed. Don't fret about it. Try having them put their hands over their eyes, or just have them keep their head and hands still.*

Q: WHAT IS A PRAYER CLOSET?

24

A: A prayer closet is a private place where a person can pray without anyone else around. It is a place where a person can get away from the busyness and noise of life. The peace and quiet helps a person spend quiet time with God, praying honestly in private without being distracted or watched by others.

A prayer closet can be a real closet where a person can shut the door, but it can also be other kinds of places. It can be a quiet spot in the house, outdoors, or somewhere else. It can be any special spot where you and God can talk. Where do you get away from everything to talk with God?

KEY VERSE: *But when you pray, go away by yourself, shut the door behind you, and pray to your Father secretly. Then your Father, who knows all secrets, will reward you. (Matthew 6:6)*

RELATED VERSES: *Matthew 14:23; Mark 1:35; Luke 5:16; 6:12*

NOTE TO PARENTS: *One of the best ways to encourage children to pray is to let them see you do it. Tell them where you like to spend time with God alone. Talk to them about your prayer times.*

Q: CAN'T WE PRAY ANYWHERE?

25

A: Yes, we can pray anywhere. Prayers do not have to be spoken aloud, so we can pray while we are sitting at a desk with our eyes wide open, or anywhere else. We can pray silently because God knows our thoughts. We can pray in school, on the playground, at basketball practice, in a choir concert, in church, at home, on vacation—anywhere! God is glad when we ask him for help right when and where we need it.

KEY VERSE: *Pray at all times and on every occasion in the power of the Holy Spirit. Stay alert and be persistent in your prayers for all Christians everywhere. (Ephesians 6:18)*

RELATED VERSES: *Isaiah 38:2; Matthew 6:5-6; Luke 5:16; 1 Peter 3:12*

RELATED QUESTION: *Where should we pray?*

NOTE TO PARENTS: *Our children can learn spontaneous prayer from us. Next time you are with the kids and you think of something you should pray about, ask them to join in and just do it briefly and naturally.*

Q: DO WE HAVE TO PRAY CERTAIN PRAYERS?

26

A: No. We do not have to pray certain prayers, but it is OK to have certain prayers that we pray often. Written prayers can be helpful. The Lord's Prayer and the Psalms, for example, are good things to pray, and they help us think of ways to pray and things we can talk to God about. Some people memorize prayers and recite them at mealtimes or at bedtime. We just need to be careful that we really mean the words as we say them. If we say them over and over again, we may not pay attention to what we are saying.

KEY VERSE: *Give thanks to the Lord and proclaim his greatness. Let the whole world know what he has done. (1 Chronicles 16:8)*

RELATED VERSES: *Psalm 13:5-6; Luke 11:2-4*

NOTE TO PARENTS: *Children will often say things a certain way or pray certain prayers because they imagine the words themselves to have power, like magic spells. Encourage your children to pray with their own words, from the heart, and not to get stuck in a pattern of praying only certain prayers. Remind them that they are talking to their heavenly Father—someone who loves them!*

Q: WHY DID JESUS SAY WE SHOULD PRAY THE LORD'S PRAYER?

LONG & FANCY PRAYERS

PRAYERS FOR VERY FORMAL OCCASIONS

IMPRESSIVE PRAYERS

THE BOOK OF LONG PRAYERS

PRAYERS TO IMPRESS PEOPLE

THE LORD'S PRAYER

THIS ONE

JESUS MADE IT SIMPLE

EASY TO PRAY

27

A:

When the disciples asked Jesus to teach them how to pray, Jesus gave them the Lord's Prayer. It is a sample prayer that shows how we should pray. In other words, it is a guide and an example, not the exact words we must say every time. It shows us a good way to pray and some good topics to pray about.

For example, it tells us that we should ask God to meet our needs. It shows us that we should pray for God's will to be done in everything that happens. And it tells us to pray that we will be strong and resist temptation. It is always good to pray that way. And it is OK for us to use our own words when we do.

KEY VERSES: *Once when Jesus had been out praying, one of his disciples came to him as he finished and said, "Lord, teach us to pray, just as John taught his disciples." He said, "This is how you should pray: Father, may your name be honored. May your Kingdom come soon. Give us our food day by day. And forgive us our sins— just as we forgive those who have sinned against us. And don't let us yield to temptation." (Luke 11:1-4)*

RELATED VERSES: *Matthew 6:9-13*

RELATED QUESTIONS: *Does God want you to always say the Lord's Prayer? Why don't they change the Lord's Prayer? Why do people say the Lord's Prayer? Why do we need to learn the Lord's Prayer? We all pray in our own way.*

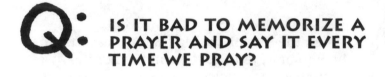

Q: IS IT BAD TO MEMORIZE A PRAYER AND SAY IT EVERY TIME WE PRAY?

28

A: It is never bad to pray a sincere and humble prayer, and memorized prayers can surely be part of that. The problem with memorized prayers is that we might get to know the prayers so well that we only say the words without thinking about them.

What matters is our attitude. Jesus wants us to say what we mean and mean what we say, not "babble on" in prayer. Our prayers should be sincere and express our true thoughts.

KEY VERSE: *When you pray, don't babble on and on as people of other religions do. They think their prayers are answered only by repeating their words again and again. (Matthew 6:7)*

RELATED VERSES: *Ecclesiastes 5:1-3*

RELATED QUESTIONS: *Why can't people pick the right words to say? Can we talk to Jesus like we talk to our friends?*

NOTE TO PARENTS: *Memorized prayers can be very inspirational and educational. Take the time to help your children understand their meaning and what they are asking. Then encourage them to add their own words on the same topic to help make the memorized prayers relevant.*

Q: DOES GOD LISTEN TO ANY PRAYER, BIG OR SMALL?

29

A: Yes, God listens to all prayers, no matter how big or small they are. In the Bible, Nehemiah prayed that he would say the right words when he talked to the king one day. Solomon prayed for wisdom. Hannah prayed for a child. Each one of these people prayed for something that mattered to him or her. It did not matter whether the prayer was big or small. They just brought their cares to God.

That is what God wants us to do. The important question is, what is on our mind? What do we care about? God will listen to any prayer if it is sincere.

KEY VERSE: *Give all your worries and cares to God, for he cares about what happens to you. (1 Peter 5:7)*

RELATED VERSES: *Nehemiah 2:4-5; Psalms 66:19; 116:1; 145:19; Proverbs 15:29*

RELATED QUESTION: *Why do you start to pray with "Dear Lord"?*

NOTE TO PARENTS: *Always encourage your children to take their concerns to God, even if those concerns seem small or simple.*

Q: WHY DO PEOPLE SAY "THEE" AND "THOU" WHEN THEY PRAY?

YEA LORD, I BESEECH THEE THAT THOU WOULDST OPEN THINE HAND AND GRANT UNTO THY SERVANT A 4×4 FULLY OPERATIONAL KIDS' JEEP WITH ALL THE ACCESSORIES.

30

A: Some people say "thee" and "thou" because they are used to it. Many years ago, the King James Version was the only English Bible. When it was written, everyone used *thee* and *thou* when they talked, so that version of the Bible has many "thees," "thous," and other words that people do not say anymore. People learned to talk to God that way because that is the way they read it in the King James Version.

Some people also feel that praying in this older style helps them show respect to God; they feel it is a more appropriate way to speak to him than to use normal language, because God is a holy and awesome God.

God wants us to talk to him in plain, everyday language. God does not care about the exact words or style of English we use as long as we say what we mean. He understands.

KEY VERSE: *Since we are receiving a Kingdom that cannot be destroyed, let us be thankful and please God by worshiping him with holy fear and awe. (Hebrews 12:28)*

RELATED VERSES: *Psalms 7:17; 47:2; 111:9; Daniel 9:4; Acts 19:17*

RELATED QUESTIONS: *If "thee" and "you" mean the same thing, why would people think God preferred them to say "thou"? How do people know God likes "thou" words? Is it all right if I say "you," or do I have to say "thee" and "thou" when I pray to God?*

NOTE TO PARENTS: *If we talk to God in plain, sincere language, our children will feel more comfortable praying than if they hear us use formal language. Using special words or tones for prayer will give them the impression that these details matter more than the content.*

Q: WHY DO WE SAY "AMEN" WHEN WE'RE DONE PRAYING?

31

A: *Amen* means "So be it" or "It is true." It is simply a way of closing a prayer. We close letters with a similar word, *sincerely. Amen* means that we have said what we mean and believe that God has heard our prayer.

To say *amen*—"So be it"—is a way of saying that we trust God to answer. It reminds us that God has everything under control.

KEY VERSE: *Blessed be the Lord, the God of Israel, from everlasting to everlasting! Let all the people say, "Amen!" Praise the Lord! (Psalm 106:48)*

RELATED VERSES: *Nehemiah 8:6; Psalm 41:13; 1 Corinthians 14:16; 2 Corinthians 1:20; Revelation 1:7*

RELATED QUESTIONS: *Do we have to say "amen" when we finish praying? Do you have to say "amen" at the end of a prayer? Why do people say "amen" while others are still praying? Does it really matter if we say "amen" at the end of our prayers? Why do some people say "amen" when I pray?*

NOTE TO PARENTS: *Be sure to explain to your children what* amen *means and that it is a declaration of their trust in God's love for them.*

WHEN
TO PRAY

32

A: The word *grace* means "thanks to God." It can also be used to mean "I ask for God's favor." This is how the apostle Paul used it to close some of his letters, such as Galatians, 1 Timothy, Philemon, and others. When we pray before meals, we are thanking God for the food and asking for his blessing on that time of eating. So this prayer is called grace.

Praying before meals is a way of showing that we depend on God. It reminds us that all we have comes from God. This is an important part of prayer— thanking God for life and everything else he gives us.

KEY VERSE: *So let us come boldly to the throne of our gracious God. There we will receive his mercy, and we will find grace to help us when we need it. (Hebrews 4:16)*

RELATED VERSES: *Romans 1:7; 16:20; Revelation 22:21*

RELATED QUESTIONS: *Why do we pray before we eat? Why do you have to say grace? Why do Christians say grace? Do we have to pray before every meal? Why do we thank God for the food?*

NOTE TO PARENTS: *Thank-you prayers are important, and it is important to teach children to include them in their prayers every day. It helps them learn that God loves and cares for them and that he is the source and owner of all they have.*

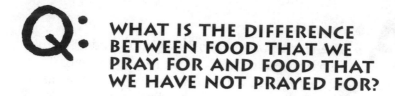

Q:

WHAT IS THE DIFFERENCE BETWEEN FOOD THAT WE PRAY FOR AND FOOD THAT WE HAVE NOT PRAYED FOR?

33

A: There is no difference between the two kinds of food. Praying at meals does not change the food. It changes us. We pray over the food to thank God for it and to ask his blessing on those who eat it, just the way Jesus did. We are saying, "God, we know that you have provided this food. We are thankful for it, and we ask you to use it to make us strong and healthy." We are asking God to bless the people at the meal.

Praying at meals reminds us that every bit of food we get comes from God's hand and that God provides everything we need.

KEY VERSE: *As they sat down to eat, he took a small loaf of bread, asked God's blessing on it, broke it, then gave it to them. (Luke 24:30)*

RELATED VERSES: *Matthew 14:19; 26:26; 1 Corinthians 10:31*

RELATED QUESTIONS: *When some people pray for food, they say, "Bless it to our bodies." Why? How come God blesses the food when he provided it? What happens if you forget to say grace before you eat? Can you pray when you're already eating? Should you pray even when you have a snack? Do we have to pray before breakfast? Do you have to pray at lunchtime? Are you supposed to pray before dinner? Is it OK to pray after the meal? Is it OK to pray in the middle of the meal? How much food can you eat before you stop to pray for it? What if someone's praying and someone's already eating? What if you have lunch with people who don't know God and they don't pray?*

WHY DO WE HAVE TO THANK GOD AT EVERY MEAL WHEN HE ALREADY KNOWS WE'RE THANKFUL?

34

A: Thanking God for food is a good habit to form because it reminds us to be thankful for all that God gives us. Sometimes we think we are thankful when we really aren't. Pausing to say thank you helps us renew our thankfulness. If we just sit down and eat without thanking God every time, we can easily and quickly forget to be thankful. We can forget that our food comes from God.

It is also a nice thing to do. We say thank you to God because he is our friend and he has done something kind for us. Don't you like it when your friends say thank you to you?

KEY VERSE: *And whatever you do or say, let it be as a representative of the Lord Jesus, all the while giving thanks through him to God the Father. (Colossians 3:17)*

RELATED VERSES: *1 Chronicles 23:30; Psalm 106:1; John 6:11; 1 Corinthians 10:30; Ephesians 5:4*

RELATED QUESTIONS: *Why do we thank God for our food? Shouldn't we thank God for the food, not our parents? Why do you thank God for your food and not your parents? Why do we thank God for food if our parents prepared it?*

NOTE TO PARENTS: *Mealtime prayer with the family is a good time for your children to start learning to pray with others. Wait until they're ready, and help them out the first few times. Take turns, and encourage adding a new prayer about something current to the regular mealtime prayer.*

Q: DO WE STILL HAVE TO THANK GOD IF WE DON'T LIKE THE FOOD?

THANK YOU, GOD, FOR THE... ER... BROCCOLI EVEN THOUGH... GULP... IT'S NOT MY FAVORITE.

A: We should thank God for our food because we need food to live and God kindly gives it to us. He meets our needs even when we are not too thrilled with the way he does it.

When we pray at meals, we do not have to say that we like the food when we really do not. But it is good to say thank you to God anyway. We need to eat. Some people have very little to eat. It only makes sense to thank God that we have a meal.

KEY VERSE: *No matter what happens, always be thankful, for this is God's will for you who belong to Christ Jesus. (1 Thessalonians 5:18)*

RELATED VERSES: *Romans 1:21; 1 Corinthians 10:30-31; Ephesians 5:4, 20; 1 Timothy 4:4-5*

RELATED QUESTIONS: *What if you have to eat something you don't like and you hide it? What about throwing your food in the garbage and someone else sees it? What if you don't like the food so you don't thank God? What if you thank God and then throw the food away?*

Q: WHY DO WE PRAY BEFORE WE GO TO BED?

DEAR GOD, PLEASE OPEN MY DAD'S EYES TO ALL THE ADVANTAGES OF LETTING ME STAY UP LONGER TO PLAY.

A: Because nighttime is a good time to pray. We can think about the day we had. We can thank God for all that he did and tell him about our problems and struggles. Also, we can pray for protection. We can ask God for a good night's sleep and for good dreams and to keep us from nightmares. Praying before going to bed is a good habit to form and keep. But not all people pray before going to bed. We can pray anytime.

KEY VERSE: *I will lie down in peace and sleep, for you alone, O Lord, will keep me safe. (Psalm 4:8)*

RELATED VERSES: *Psalms 42:8; 55:16-17; 119:62; 141:2*

RELATED QUESTIONS: *Why do people pray at night instead of in the daytime? Doesn't God sleep? Is it wrong to go to sleep without praying just because you don't know what to pray about? Why would you pray only at night?*

NOTE TO PARENTS: *Nighttime is a good time to teach your children to pray. It gives you an opportunity to set aside a regular, special, quiet-time of prayer without a lot of distractions. It lets you model how to pray and what kinds of concerns to bring to God. And it lets you review how God has blessed you as a family that day.*

Q: WHY DO WE HAVE TO PRAY WHEN WE DON'T WANT TO?

37

A: Eating foods that are good for us, brushing our teeth, getting up when the alarm goes off, working hard in school, practicing the piano, and cleaning up our messes are all good. We are glad we did them after they are done, but often we do them only because they need to be done, not because they are fun.

God tells us to pray because it draws us closer to God. It changes us. It helps us understand God's will better. It helps us give our worries to God. So we should pray even when we do not feel like it.

If we wait until we feel like praying, we may never do it. This is true of all good activities, not just prayer. We have to work at things that are good and important. But the rewards are always worth it.

KEY VERSE: *No discipline is enjoyable while it is happening—it is painful! But afterward there will be a quiet harvest of right living for those who are trained in this way. (Hebrews 12:11)*

RELATED VERSES: *Luke 22:46; Romans 12:12; Colossians 4:2; 1 Peter 4:7*

RELATED QUESTIONS: *What if you don't like to pray? Why should you pray if you're angry? Should you pray when you're scared? Should you pray when you have a bad dream? Why do people think God won't hear you when you're angry? What if your brother's baby-sitting you and doesn't want to pray?*

NOTE TO PARENTS: *It is important to make learning fun. But children need to understand that we pray not because it is fun but because it is vital to life. Our relationship with God is life's foundation, and prayer is the key to that relationship.*

Q: WHY DO WE HAVE TO GIVE THANKS FOR THINGS WE DON'T LIKE?

38

A: God tells us to thank him *in* all things, not *for* all things. That means that when something bad happens, we should thank God for being there with us through those bad times. This helps us remember that God is in control and that he still loves us and has a plan for us, no matter what happens.

We do not have to thank God for bad events. If something bad happens, it is bad. God does not ask us to be glad for that. Maybe a pet or a relative died. That is a bad thing, and it is OK to cry about it.

But God also tells us to be grateful for him and his plan. Some of the things we do not like are actually good for us. Maybe it is good even if we do not like it. Or maybe God has a plan that we cannot see. We need to trust in God's goodness; that is why we thank him in all things.

KEY VERSE: *Whatever you do or say, let it be as a representative of the Lord Jesus, all the while giving thanks through him to God the Father. (Colossians 3:17)*

RELATED VERSES: *Psalms 69:30; 100:4; Ephesians 5:4, 20*

RELATED QUESTIONS: *Why do you have to thank God for things that you don't want? Why do we thank God? Does God always want us to be happy with what he does? Even if we get hurt bad, do we thank God for it? I think that thanking and worshiping God is the best part of prayer, right? Is it wrong to not be thankful when God gives us something we don't want? Should you thank God for stuff?*

Q: WHY SHOULD WE GO TO GOD FOR HELP?

39

A: We should ask God for help because we need him. Asking why we should go to God for help is like asking "Why should I go to the gas station for gas?" God is the one who gives us life, the one who makes us able to walk, talk, and move; he is the one who gives us knowledge and the one who gives us all we need. In a sense, he is the *only* one who can help us. That is why we should go to God for help.

KEY VERSE: *In my distress I prayed to the Lord, and the Lord answered me and rescued me. (Psalm 118:5)*

RELATED VERSES: *Psalms 17:6; 118:7-9; 144:2; Hebrews 13:6*

RELATED QUESTIONS: *If someone's in trouble and not praying, should you pray for them? Do we pray when we need to?*

NOTE TO PARENTS: *The world does not teach children to recognize God as their source of help. They will need to learn it from you. Point your children to God in prayer as the first stop on the way to getting help and finding answers.*

Q: WHY DO PEOPLE WAIT UNTIL THE LAST MINUTE TO PRAY?

40

A: Some people wait till the last minute to pray because they forget or because they do not think they need God's help. They rely on themselves so much that they think they can do almost anything on their own. Or they may have forgotten about God. Then, when things get worse, they cry out to God for help as a last resort.

Instead of doing those things, we should remember that we need God's help all the time. We should talk with him *first* in every situation we face.

Of course, we should not wait until we have a huge problem to pray. We should talk with God about everything. We should praise the Lord every day because it reminds us that he is there, he loves us, and he is in charge of everything that happens. That helps us avoid a lot of problems in the first place.

KEY VERSE: *Praise the Lord, I tell myself, and never forget the good things he does for me. (Psalm 103:2)*

RELATED VERSES: *Deuteronomy 6:12; Psalms 107:12-13, 18-19, 25-28; 118:8-9; 119:93; Colossians 4:2; 2 Peter 3:5*

RELATED QUESTION: *Why do people only pray when they have a problem?*

NOTE TO PARENTS: *People begin to grow in prayer when they turn to God during times of calm. Pray together with your children even when you have everything you need. This will help them mature in their prayer habits.*

Q: WHAT HAPPENS IF WE DON'T PRAY AT ALL?

41

A: People who do not pray at all grow distant from God, like friends who grow apart because they never talk to each other. Friends keep their friendship close by talking with each other. People who never talk to each other become almost like strangers. People who do not pray miss out on getting to know God better.

Also, people who do not pray miss out on God's help. It is the people who call out to God who get to see God work most. They see him change things and people in awesome ways. They learn things that they could not have learned on their own. People who do not pray cut themselves off from this special part of God's plan.

We need to stay close to God, and we need his power. Prayer meets those needs.

KEY VERSE: *[Jesus said,] "And so I tell you, keep on asking, and you will be given what you ask for. Keep on looking, and you will find. Keep on knocking, and the door will be opened." (Luke 11:9)*

RELATED VERSES: *1 Samuel 12:23; Psalms 14:4-5; 120:1; Matthew 26:41; James 5:16*

RELATED QUESTIONS: *How can people have so many prayers? How would we know to pray for someone if we didn't know they needed it? Should you always pray to God if you have any questions? Why should we pray when we feel we should?*

NOTE TO PARENTS: *We need to be very clear with our children on this issue. God will not force himself into our lives. It is not true that a person can walk with God without prayer. Prayer is God's plan and program for having a relationship with him.*

WHAT HAPPENS IF WE'RE INTERRUPTED WHEN WE'RE PRAYING?

42

A: It is just like a conversation with somebody else—we stop until we can pick up where we left off later. Of course, if we keep getting interrupted in our prayers, we should try to find a place and time where we can pray without any distractions. But it is OK to start praying again if we get interrupted in the middle of a prayer.

KEY VERSE: *Jesus often withdrew to the wilderness for prayer. (Luke 5:16)*

RELATED VERSES: *Mark 1:35; Acts 10:9; 1 Peter 4:7*

RELATED QUESTIONS: *What about being distracted while you're praying?*

Q: WHAT DOES "PRAYING CONTINUALLY" MEAN?

43

A: When the Bible talks about praying continually, it means always being ready to pray. It means checking in with God throughout the day. It means that our *first* response when something happens is to pray. When something bad happens, we ask for help. When something good happens, we thank God. When we do not know what to do, we ask God to give us wisdom. It means talking to him as a friend and as a loving Father who is always around.

When you think about it, it makes perfect sense. God *is* our Friend and loving Father who is always around!

KEY VERSE: *Keep on praying. (1 Thessalonians 5:17)*

RELATED VERSES: *Ephesians 6:18; 2 Timothy 1:3*

RELATED QUESTIONS: *How many times should you pray a day? How often should we pray? Why don't people pray all the time? When it says "pray continually," does it mean you have to pray every hour? Why do we have to pray continually? Should we always pray? Will God still love us?*

NOTE TO PARENTS: *Our children need to know that we pray because of our relationship with God. We pray to get to know him better and to develop our relationship with him. That is prayer's purpose. Do not leave your children with the impression that prayer is always a dry time of merely covering the day's issues.*

Q: DOES PRAYING A LOT MAKE A PERSON BETTER?

44

A: Yes. Praying a lot makes a person better because it draws that person closer to God. Prayer makes a person more sensitive to God's will, to others, and to what is important. Praying gets the focus off one's self and onto God. When we spend time with God, we become more like him, just the way we become more like the friends we hang around with.

We just need to be careful not to compare ourselves with others. We need to concentrate on praying more, not on praying more than someone else we know.

KEY VERSE: *Devote yourselves to prayer with an alert mind and a thankful heart. (Colossians 4:2)*

RELATED VERSES: *Psalm 77:11-12; Acts 2:42; 1 Thessalonians 3:10; James 5:16; 1 Peter 3:12*

RELATED QUESTIONS: *Am I supposed to pray every day? Why do we have to pray every day? Do we need to pray more than once every day? Can I just pray grace every day?*

NOTE TO PARENTS: *Longer prayers come from sincere conversation with God, not from a concern with longer prayers. Let your children grow in prayer as a result of their growing relationship with God. Do not focus on how many minutes they spend praying each day.*

Q: CAN WE PRAY ANYTIME WE WANT?

45

A: Yes, we can pray to God anytime we want. God does not mind if we pray between meals, after bedtime prayer (when we can't sleep), or in school. Because of Christ, the door to God is always open. We can always go to him.

Of course, we need to respect others. We should not start praying out loud in the middle of a conversation with our friends. But if we are in a group, we can still take a moment to pray silently if we need to.

KEY VERSE: *Pray at all times and on every occasion in the power of the Holy Spirit. Stay alert and be persistent in your prayers for all Christians everywhere. (Ephesians 6:18)*

RELATED VERSES: *Psalm 86:3; Colossians 4:2*

RELATED QUESTIONS: *Why are there special times to pray? What is the best time to pray? What are the special times that it's good to pray? Should you pray on holidays? Do people pray every day and every night? How come you have to pray every day? What if you don't pray for a whole year? When should we pray?*

NOTE TO PARENTS: *Keep affirming how pleased God is with your children when they pray and how much he loves to talk to them. We want to spend time with the people we love, and so does God. He is pleased when his children come to him in prayer.*

WHAT TO PRAY FOR

Q: WHAT DO WE NEED TO PRAY FOR?

46

A: We need to pray for three things: (1) our needs, (2) the needs of others, and (3) God's will to be done. Many of the requests we bring to God will be one of these kinds of prayers.

For example, we need food, clothing, and shelter. So do other people. We also need forgiveness, and help in resisting temptation, doing good, and becoming what God wants us to be.

We also need to pray for God's will to be done on earth. Jesus taught us to pray, "May your will be done here on earth, just as it is in heaven" (Matthew 6:10). This is also one reason the Bible tells us to pray for leaders. We can affect events in the world by praying this way.

We do not have to limit our prayers to needs. We can praise God and tell him how wonderful he is. God is our friend. He wants to hear from us.

KEY VERSES: *He said, "This is how you should pray: Father, may your name be honored. May your Kingdom come soon. Give us our food day by day. And forgive us our sins—just as we forgive those who have sinned against us. And don't let us yield to temptation." (Luke 11:2-4)*

RELATED VERSES: *Luke 11:9-10; John 16:23-24; Philippians 4:6; 1 Timothy 2:1-4*

RELATED QUESTIONS: *Does God sometimes tell us what to pray for? Why do we have to pray for things? Do you have to ask God for stuff?*

NOTE TO PARENTS: *You can introduce your children to different prayer needs one at a time. When they get a handle on one, you can move them on to the next. That way they have time to learn each one well.*

47

A: If something is important to us, we should feel free to pray about it. God does not laugh at people when they pray. He does not have a list of topics that people should not pray about.

Prayer is one of the main ways God changes people for the better. If there is something wrong with the way we are praying, God will reveal it to us in a kind way. In fact, our prayer will draw us closer to God, and he will use our relationship with him to help us change. Of course, prayer should be sincere, not silly or selfish. But God will not make fun of us for talking to him about this or that topic. He will always listen to what we have to say.

It would not make sense to ask God to do something that is wrong or bad, because God never sins. But we can talk to God about anything that concerns us.

KEY VERSE: *Let us come boldly to the throne of our gracious God. There we will receive his mercy, and we will find grace to help us when we need it. (Hebrews 4:16)*

RELATED VERSES: *Matthew 7:7-11; John 14:13-14*

RELATED QUESTIONS: *Why can't we pray for other stuff besides good health and protection? Does God care what we pray about? Can you pray it would rain gold? Can you pray for animals to talk? If you are captive with the police, are you allowed to pray that you can break free?*

NOTE TO PARENTS: *Concentrate on teaching your children to turn to God in prayer as a way of life, not on restricting their prayers to a certain type. It is much more important that they develop the habit of prayer than that they "get it perfect" at a young age.*

Q: CAN WE TELL GOD EVERYTHING WE WANT TO?

48

A: Yes, we can talk to God about any joy, sorrow, need, feeling, worry, doubt, or fear that is on our mind. It is important to be honest with God and say what we are thinking.

But whenever we are angry or upset, we should also try to remember that God is on our side. Job did this when he was hurt and confused. He told God how he felt, but he did not accuse God of doing something wrong just because he was so upset. He knew God was good and loved him, so Job did not take out his anger on God. David's psalms are this way too; Psalm 22 is a good example. If we are hurt or angry, we should tell God, but we should also say that we know he is good. We can also ask him to help us understand and trust him. We should not accuse God of evil or of doing bad things.

KEY VERSES: *Don't worry about anything; instead, pray about everything. Tell God what you need, and thank him for all he has done. If you do this, you will experience God's peace, which is far more wonderful than the human mind can understand. His peace will guard your hearts and minds as you live in Christ Jesus. (Philippians 4:6-7)*

RELATED VERSES: *Job 1:20-22; 2:9-10; Psalms 22:16-24; 139:23-24; 1 Timothy 4:4-5*

RELATED QUESTIONS: *Can we pray to ask God how old he is? If you pray, how many awards will you get in heaven? Is it bad to not pray for some things you already know about?*

NOTE TO PARENTS: *Help your children talk openly with God, just like they do with people they trust when they feel deeply about something. But also encourage them to be ready to learn and change.*

Q: DOES GOD WANT US TO PRAY FOR OUR FRIENDS?

49

A: God definitely wants us to pray for our friends. John 17 tells about Jesus praying for his disciples. He prayed that they would be filled with joy, made holy, unified, and protected from the evil one. Jesus thought that it was important to pray for his friends in this way.

We can also pray for our friends' problems, their attitude, that they will come to know Jesus, and that they learn to be better friends. In fact, this is one way we keep them as friends. Whatever our friends need, we can pray for them, and God welcomes such prayers.

KEY VERSE: *I urge you, first of all, to pray for all people. As you make your requests, plead for God's mercy upon them, and give thanks. (1 Timothy 2:1)*

RELATED VERSES: *Matthew 5:43-48; John 17:6-26*

RELATED QUESTIONS: *Can you pray for friends? Can we pray for kindness and love? Can you pray for your friends not to get in trouble? Can you pray for kids that don't play with you?*

NOTE TO PARENTS: *Guide your children in praying for a friend each night.*

Q: CAN WE PRAY FOR ANIMALS?

50

A: We can pray about anything that is important to us, and that includes animals. God wants us to talk with him about the things that matter to us. He is our friend, and he cares about us. Also, God created the animals, and he loves them. So if an animal or a pet is important to us, we should feel free to pray for it. Certainly farmers should pray for their animals.

KEY VERSE: *The godly are concerned for the welfare of their animals. (Proverbs 12:10)*

RELATED VERSES: *Psalm 104:10-23; Matthew 6:26; Luke 12:24*

RELATED QUESTIONS: *Can we pray for pets? Can you pray your pets would listen to you?*

Q: DO WE HAVE TO PRAY FOR PEOPLE WE HAVEN'T MET BEFORE?

51

A: We do not have to meet people in order to pray for them. For example, the Bible tells us to pray for government leaders. Surely we have not met all the leaders of the country, but we should pray for them anyway. We should also pray for missionaries we hear or know about, even if we have never met them. So, yes, we should pray for some of the people we have never met before.

Remember that prayer can be an adventure. We can affect decisions of the president or mayor by praying for that person. Try not to look at it as a duty or a job but as a privilege. It is kind of like helping run the country.

KEY VERSES: *Pray this way for kings and all others who are in authority, so that we can live in peace and quietness, in godliness and dignity. This is good and pleases God our Savior, for he wants everyone to be saved and to understand the truth. (1 Timothy 2:2-4)*

RELATED VERSES: *Romans 8:26-27; 15:30; Ephesians 6:18; 1 Timothy 2:1*

RELATED QUESTIONS: *Can you pray for people in other places in the world? Can we pray that God would give us enough food to give to the poor? Would God want me to pray for people that have no home? Why do we pray for other people? Can you pray for other people?*

NOTE TO PARENTS: *From time to time, lead your children in praying for people they know; then, guide them to include someone they don't know. God will help them learn to pray beyond their own experience. After all, prayer is a dialogue with God, and he will teach them as they practice and get to know him better.*

Q: CAN WE PRAY FOR MONEY?

52

A: Most certainly. We need money to survive, and God wants us to rely on him to meet our needs. So it is wise and good to pray for money and for the means to earn it.

One of the best ways to pray for money is to ask God to help us earn or work for the money we need. God may answer a prayer for money by providing a job or a gift. Or he may teach us to get by with less. When we pray for money, we should be willing to accept whatever answer God gives.

We should ask God to show us how we can use what we have more wisely. If we make better use of what we earn, we may not need any more. Sometimes God provides for us by making us better money managers.

We need to heed one caution: God says that we may not get what we ask for if we only want to spend it on our own pleasures. So when we ask God for money, we should think about how we can give some to the church and share some with others.

KEY VERSES: *You parents—if your children ask for a loaf of bread, do you give them a stone instead? Or if they ask for a fish, do you give them a snake? Of course not! If you sinful people know how to give good gifts to your children, how much more will your heavenly Father give good gifts to those who ask him. (Matthew 7:9-11)*

RELATED VERSES: *Proverbs 30:8; Matthew 6:11*

RELATED QUESTIONS: *Can we pray for things we want? Is it OK to pray for lots and lots of things? Is it OK to pray for all there is? Instead of praying for specific things, why don't you just pray for a good day and thank God for everything he did for us?*

Q: CAN WE ASK GOD TO GIVE US THINGS LIKE TOYS?

53

A: It is all right to ask God for fun things such as toys. We can talk with God about anything. But praying for something does not mean that we will get it. God knows if something is good or bad for us. He may not give us something because it is not good for us.

The Bible warns us that we should not ask God for things if we want them only for selfish reasons. Solomon knew this. God promised to give Solomon whatever he asked for. Solomon decided to ask for wisdom. God was very pleased with this. He said Solomon made the right choice because he did not ask for great wealth or power. Then God rewarded him by making him rich and powerful.

Ask for things that help others. God wants us to trust him to meet our needs.

KEY VERSES: *God said to Solomon, "Because your greatest desire is to help your people, and you did not ask for personal wealth and honor or the death of your enemies or even a long life, but rather you asked for wisdom and knowledge to properly govern my people, I will certainly give you the wisdom and knowledge you requested. And I will also give you riches, wealth, and honor such as no other king has ever had before you or will ever have again!" (2 Chronicles 1:11-12)*

RELATED VERSES: *James 4:1-3*

RELATED QUESTIONS: *Is it OK to ask for something? Does God want you to pray for the toy you wanted?*

NOTE TO PARENTS: *Help your children look to God, not things, as the source of happiness. Whenever they want to pray for toys or other fun things, guide them to ask God to do what he thinks best. This is part of teaching them to trust God to rule in their lives.*

Q: IS IT OK TO PRAY TO GET SOMETHING THAT OUR FRIENDS HAVE?

DEAR GOD, PLEASE GIVE ME FREDA'S SENSE OF HUMOR, GOOD VALUES LIKE SUSIE'S, AND A BASEBALL CARD COLLECTION LIKE TOMMY'S.

54

A: It is good to tell God what is on our mind, but it is not good to think that we need to have certain things to be happy. Having things does not make us happy. God knows this. So we should not think that if we suddenly had a new toy or piece of clothing we would be happy forever. Knowing God and obeying him is what makes us happy.

Craving what others have is called envy. God tells us not to envy because people who envy are never satisfied; they never think they have enough, even after they get all that they want. Instead of envying, God tells us to be content with what we have.

But we should still tell God how we feel. When a friend has something that we would like, we should talk with God about it, especially if it is something that we need. Then we should trust that God will give us what is best for us.

KEY VERSE: *Do not covet your neighbor's house. Do not covet your neighbor's wife, male or female servant, ox or donkey, or anything else your neighbor owns. (Exodus 20:17)*

RELATED VERSES: *1 Samuel 8:5-20; James 4:1-3*

RELATED QUESTIONS: *Can you ask for your friends' stuff? Is it wrong to ask God to give other people candy? Is it OK to pray for more of what you already have?*

NOTE TO PARENTS: *Make sure your children know about advertising and how it works. If they can learn to recognize the hard sell, they will be more prepared to handle it correctly.*

Q: IS IT BAD TO ASK GOD FOR SOMETHING WE DON'T REALLY NEED?

55

A: It is not the *best* way to pray, but it is not bad. God invites us to come to him with our needs and concerns. He invites us to tell him how we feel. He promises to meet our needs, to care about our cares, and to work out his good plan in our lives.

That means we should ask him to meet our true needs and talk to him about our problems. It does not mean we should treat God like Santa Claus and always be asking for a long list of things that we want only for ourselves.

Sometimes we ask God for things that we *think* we need, but really we do not need them at all. It is OK to tell God we wish we had this or that thing. Whenever we pray, we should be honest and tell God our real feelings. But we should accept his answers and be content with what he gives us.

KEY VERSES: *I know how to live on almost nothing or with everything. I have learned the secret of living in every situation, whether it is with a full stomach or empty, with plenty or little. For I can do everything with the help of Christ who gives me the strength I need. (Philippians 4:12-13)*

RELATED VERSES: *Matthew 6:31-33; 7:11; Philippians 4:19*

RELATED QUESTIONS: *Can we pray for dirt bikes? Can we pray for new clothes? Can we pray for a rocket? Can we pray for a new car? Will God buy Dad a new Jeep?*

NOTE TO PARENTS: *Listen to your children's heart when they ask a question like this. Some children need encouragement to ask God for anything, and others come to prayer time with a long list. Encourage a balance, and, most important, teach kids to trust in God.*

IF WE PRAYED TO FIND
SOMETHING WE LOST, WOULD
WE REALLY FIND IT?

56

A: If it was part of God's plan for us, yes. No job is too small for God. It is good to pray for what matters to us, even something small that is lost. God may help us find it right away, or he may help us remember where we put it. He also might have us retrace our steps to find it so we will be more careful next time.

But prayer does not substitute for being careful. We should not be careless and think, "Oh, well, if I lose it, I can just ask God to find it for me." That would be using prayer the wrong way.

KEY VERSES: *As one of them was chopping, his ax head fell into the river. "Ah, my lord!" he cried. "It was a borrowed ax!" "Where did it fall?" the man of God asked. When he showed him the place, Elisha cut a stick and threw it into the water. Then the ax head rose to the surface and floated. (2 Kings 6:5-6)*

RELATED VERSES: *Psalm 139:1-2; Matthew 10:29-31; Luke 15:8*

RELATED QUESTIONS: *How does God help you find things when you lose them? When you've lost a little key, can you pray to find it? If someone stole your car, can you pray that you'll get it back?*

NOTE TO PARENTS: *Let your children hear you pray aloud, in both small matters and big ones. Also talk with them about God's answers. This will help them see how God works in your life and, therefore, in theirs.*

WHAT IF KIDS ARE MEAN TO
US AND IT'S HARD FOR US TO
PRAY FOR THEM?

57

A: It is not always easy to pray. But praying for kids who are mean to us is one of the best things we can do to help them. We can pray that God will help those who are mean to stop being mean. We can also pray that God will help us to be kind and loving to them so they will learn about God's love through our example. Maybe if they see God's love in us, they will come to know Jesus.

We should let God judge others. In other words, we should not pray for God to punish someone, even our enemies. Instead, we should pray that people will trust in Jesus and that they will develop a love for God. If they love God, they will stop being mean.

KEY VERSES: *[Jesus said,] "But if you are willing to listen, I say, love your enemies. Do good to those who hate you. Pray for the happiness of those who curse you. Pray for those who hurt you." (Luke 6:27-28)*

RELATED VERSES: *Matthew 5:43-48; 1 Timothy 2:8*

RELATED QUESTIONS: *What if you don't want to pray for someone? Why do we have to pray for people who are mean to us? What if people beat you up? Do you still have to pray for them? Do we have to pray for people who hate us? Does God really expect you to pray for good things to happen to bad kids, and meanwhile they still hate you? What do you do if you don't want to love and pray for your enemies? Should you pray for others even though you don't like them? Why would Jesus say to pray for our enemies who do mean things to us, if he wants us to love ourselves?*

58

A: The main reason to pray for our enemies is because God tells us to. In fact, he tells us to *love* our enemies. Praying for our enemies and loving them is God's way.

Another reason is that all people, especially bad people, need prayer. There is no better way to change them. If we want bad people to stop being bad, we need to ask God to do it. We need to pray for them so that they will change.

Jesus prayed for his enemies. He prayed for the religious leaders who wanted him to die, and he prayed for us. He did that because he loved us, even while we were God's enemies.

KEY VERSES: *But I say, love your enemies! Pray for those who persecute you! In that way, you will be acting as true children of your Father in heaven. For he gives his sunlight to both the evil and the good, and he sends rain on the just and on the unjust, too. (Matthew 5:44-45)*

RELATED VERSES: *Psalm 109:4-5; Luke 6:27-28; Romans 12:14, 19-20*

RELATED QUESTIONS: *Even if enemies kill someone you like, do you have to pray for them? Why can't we ask God to punish our enemies? Why should we pray for our enemies? If we pray for them, they'll pick on us more. Is it wrong to not pray for people you hate? If we pray for someone everyone hates, what should we do when they start hating us? Why do you have to love your enemies? Does God want us to pray for evil people?*

Q: CAN WE ASK GOD TO HELP US PASS A TEST?

59

A: We can ask God for help on a test because we can talk with God about anything. But God expects us to do our best at whatever we do. We go to school and work as part of his plan to grow us into adults. It is true that we rely on God for strength, wisdom, and life. But that is not the same as asking God to live our lives for us.

We should do our duty as students. We should study for tests and do what the teacher says. Then we should pray and ask God to give us a clear mind to take the test as well as we can, to help us relax, and to remember what we have studied.

God is merciful, and he does help us. But it helps to study for the test more than to pray for God to rescue us from a lack of studying. We can ask God to help us study.

KEY VERSES: *Work hard and cheerfully at whatever you do, as though you were working for the Lord rather than for people. Remember that the Lord will give you an inheritance as your reward, and the Master you are serving is Christ. (Colossians 3:23-24)*

RELATED VERSES: *Psalms 34:15; 55:16; Ephesians 6:18; Philippians 4:6-7; 2 Timothy 2:15*

RELATED QUESTIONS: *Could you pray for help on memorizing your verse? If we studied hard on a test, do we still have to ask God to help us to pass the test? Will God help me pass my test if I didn't study? Can you pray for the memory and study yourself? Can we pray for anything? Even good math marks? Is it wrong to not study for a test and ask for God's help?*

Q:
WHEN WE'RE SAD, CAN WE PRAY THAT SOMEONE WILL COME PLAY WITH US?

60

A: Yes. God cares for us, he wants us to have good friends, and he wants to comfort us when we are sad. Those are the three main reasons that it is OK to ask God to send someone to play with us when we are sad. We can talk with God about anything. It is especially important to be honest and tell him how we are feeling.

We can also pray that we can be a friend and a comfort to someone else. Maybe someone nearby is feeling lonely and needs a friend. Sometimes the best way to get a friend is to be a friend.

KEY VERSE: *Please keep a guest room ready for me, for I am hoping that God will answer your prayers and let me return to you soon. (Philemon 1:22)*

RELATED VERSE: *Hebrews 13:19*

RELATED QUESTIONS: *Is it selfish to only pray for yourself? Is it selfish to pray to be rich? Can you ask for stuff for free? When I'm lost, can I pray?*

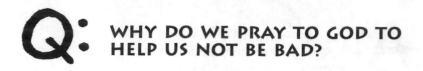

Q: WHY DO WE PRAY TO GOD TO HELP US NOT BE BAD?

61

A: Because we all sin. It is natural for us to do bad things. So we need God's help to do good things instead of bad. God can help us, and he wants to. In fact, God is the only one who has the power to help us overcome temptation.

When the disciples asked Jesus how to pray, he gave them what we call the Lord's Prayer. In that prayer he taught them to pray, "Don't let us yield to temptation, but deliver us from the evil one." When we pray a prayer like that, we ask God to help us not be bad.

KEY VERSE: *And don't let us yield to temptation, but deliver us from the evil one. (Matthew 6:13)*

RELATED VERSES: *Psalms 51:3; 139:23-24; 2 Corinthians 13:7, 9; Ephesians 6:19*

RELATED QUESTIONS: *Is it wrong to not pray for something that needs prayer? If we do something bad, can we pray about it?*

Q: WHY DO WE ASK JESUS INTO OUR HEART?

62

A: When we say "heart," we mean the part of us that decides everything. So when someone says that we ought to ask Jesus into our heart, the person means that we should ask Jesus to be the true master of our lives. It also means that we ask him to be our Savior, to forgive our sins, and to take care of us. That is how a person becomes a Christian. When we do this, the Holy Spirit really does come and live inside us. Then we have him with us all the time.

KEY VERSE: *I pray that Christ will be more and more at home in your hearts as you trust in him. May your roots go down deep into the soil of God's marvelous love. (Ephesians 3:17)*

RELATED VERSES: *John 16:5-7; Acts 15:8-9; 16:14; 28:26-27; Romans 5:5; 10:8-10; 2 Corinthians 3:3; Galatians 4:6-7; Revelation 3:20*

RELATED QUESTIONS: *Is Jesus knocking on your heart to let him in? How do people become Christians? Should I ask God to forgive me for my sins in general, or say each sin I have done and ask him to forgive me? Can Satan change your heart back to a black heart? Can God keep it white?*

NOTE TO PARENTS: *Whenever a question like this comes up, be prepared to talk about your children's own decision to accept Jesus. Be ready and willing to invite them to pray to receive Christ if they have never done so before.*

Q: DO WE HAVE TO PRAY TO BE FORGIVEN?

DEAR GOD, PLEASE FORGIVE ME FOR THE THINGS I DID WRONG TODAY. AND WOULD IT BE TOO MUCH TO ASK YOU TO FORGIVE ME IN ADVANCE FOR ALL THE MISTAKES I'LL PROBABLY MAKE TOMORROW?

63

A: Whenever we ask God to forgive us, he forgives us. That is what the word *confession* means. It means that we tell God what we have done, agree with him that it is wrong, and ask him to forgive us. Because only God can forgive sins, we need to confess them to him in order to be truly forgiven. And we have his promise that he will always forgive if we come to him truly sorry for what we have done.

KEY VERSE: *If we confess our sins to him, he is faithful and just to forgive us and to cleanse us from every wrong. (1 John 1:9)*

RELATED VERSES: *Psalms 25:11; 32:1-6; 51:1-19; Matthew 6:12, 14-15; Mark 11:25*

RELATED QUESTIONS: *If you don't pray, do you still go to heaven? If you pray to God, will he give you better permission to go to heaven? Why did Jesus die?*

NOTE TO PARENTS: *There is no better way to teach children about confession than to show them how it is done. Always be willing to seek out forgiveness if appropriate, and let your children hear you confess sins to God.*

Q: CAN GOD HELP US PRAY?

64

A: Yes. Many times we want to talk with God but just don't know what to say or how to put our feelings into words. The Holy Spirit can help us think of the right words and say them. But even if we still don't know what to say, God knows what we are feeling and thinking. He knows that we sincerely want to talk with him, and he understands what we *would* say if we could.

The best way to pray is just to pray. That is, we should not wait until we think we have all the right words. We should just speak to God from the heart as best we can. He will understand what we mean even if we get the words messed up.

KEY VERSES: *The Holy Spirit helps us in our distress. For we don't even know what we should pray for, nor how we should pray. But the Holy Spirit prays for us with groanings that cannot be expressed in words. And the Father who knows all hearts knows what the Spirit is saying, for the Spirit pleads for us believers in harmony with God's own will. (Romans 8:26-27)*

RELATED VERSES: *Hebrews 7:25; 1 Peter 5:7*

RELATED QUESTIONS: *Why does the Holy Spirit pray for us? Does Jesus help you pray? How does God pray with us when we're praying? How would we know to pray for someone if we didn't know they needed it?*

NOTE TO PARENTS: *Encourage your children to pray even if they do not feel that they are good at it. Remind them that God is gentle and kind and always ready to hear their prayers and that God will never make fun of them for how they pray.*

ANSWERS TO PRAYERS

Q: HOW CAN GOD HEAR OUR PRAYERS FROM HEAVEN?

65

A: God can do anything. He is all-powerful and unlimited. He is everywhere all the time. He also knows everything. He knows what we think as well as what we say. So God can hear everyone's prayers from all over the world all the time.

Sometimes people think that God is "out there in heaven," far away. But God is not far away; he is always right here with us, living among his people.

KEY VERSE: *I am the Lord, the God of all the peoples of the world. Is anything too hard for me? (Jeremiah 32:27)*

RELATED VERSES: *Psalms 18:6; 116:1-2; 130:2; 139:2, 17-18*

RELATED QUESTIONS: *How does God listen? How does God hear prayers? Does God hear us when we pray? How can God hear what we say?*

Q: IF WE TALK TO GOD, DOES HE ALWAYS HEAR US?

66

A: Yes, God *always* hears us, no matter where we are or what we are doing. He is never asleep or far away. Nothing can stop him from hearing what we say.

God knows our thoughts, too. We do not have to talk loudly so that he can hear us. Even if we barely whisper or just think our prayer, God hears us.

But we also need to know that God hates sin. If we keep sin in our heart and try to hide it, God will want us to confess it first. He will hear our prayer, but he will be waiting to hear us confess our sin first. Then he will listen to our requests.

God loves us more than we could possibly imagine. He *wants* to hear from us. He is always available and always listening. We can talk to him anytime throughout the day.

KEY VERSES: *If I had not confessed the sin in my heart, my Lord would not have listened. But God did listen! He paid attention to my prayer. Praise God, who did not ignore my prayer and did not withdraw his unfailing love from me. (Psalm 66:18-20)*

RELATED VERSES: *Proverbs 15:29; Isaiah 55:6-7; 59:1-2; 1 Peter 3:12*

RELATED QUESTIONS: *Does God listen to you when you pray? Does God always hear you? Doesn't God always listen to our prayers? God is always listening, right?*

NOTE TO PARENTS: *Always present the positive side of what God knows, not just the negative. While it is true that the wicked cannot hide from God, it is just as true that God's people never have to fear his inattention. God is always ready and willing to hear our prayers. Comfort your children with this fact.*

HOW DOES GOD CONCENTRATE ON MILLIONS OF PEOPLE ALL PRAYING AT ONCE?

67

A: God is unlimited and all-powerful. He has no trouble hearing everyone's prayers all at once. Even human beings can do two things at once. People can ride a bike and notice things in the neighborhood at the same time. Yet God is far, far bigger and stronger than we are; he can easily do a million things at once. Also, he is everywhere at all times, and he knows everything. He knows what we think as well as what we say.

Always try to remember that we are different from God. He made us to be in one place at a time. He made us to think about one thing at a time. God is not limited in that way.

KEY VERSES: *What mighty praise, O God, belongs to you in Zion. We will fulfill our vows to you, for you answer our prayers, and to you all people will come. (Psalm 65:1-2)*

RELATED VERSES: *Psalm 139:4-6; Jeremiah 32:27; Romans 11:33-34*

RELATED QUESTIONS: *How can God hear so many people all at once? Doesn't it get a little noisy in his brain? Does God get headaches from everyone talking to him? Is he always listening? How can God give answers to everyone's prayers at once? How can God answer all the prayers if he's up in heaven?*

NOTE TO PARENTS: *It is important for our children to understand that the number of people who talk to God all at once does not diminish the amount of love and personal attention he gives each one. God is so awesome that when we pray we have his full love and attentiveness.*

Q: DOES GOD USUALLY GIVE US WHAT WE PRAY FOR?

68

A:

Sometimes we pray for things that will hurt us or others, or we pray with a selfish attitude. It would not be good if God gave us what we asked for in those situations. At other times, what we want is good but not part of God's plan for us. Sometimes God wants us to wait—he may give us what we ask for, but not now. He knows that later is better.

But at other times, God does give us what we ask for because it is a good thing, and God loves to give us good things.

God has already told us how he will answer certain kinds of prayers. He promises to give us what we ask for whenever we ask for food, clothing, help living the Christian life, and wisdom. On the other hand, we know God will answer no whenever we ask for things that go against his will. We can be sure that God will always do what is best.

KEY VERSES: *He [Jesus] walked away, about a stone's throw, and knelt down and prayed, "Father, if you are willing, please take this cup of suffering away from me. Yet I want your will, not mine." (Luke 22:41-42)*

RELATED VERSES: *Psalm 17:6; Isaiah 55:8-9; Matthew 6:10; 7:11; Romans 11:36; James 1:5; 4:13-17*

RELATED QUESTIONS: *How many wishes do we get? Will God give you things from heaven that you wished for? Would God give somebody a home if they were poor? Would God supply me a home when I don't have one?*

NOTE TO PARENTS: *Encourage your children to ask God for specific things they are concerned about and to ask God for his will. Then encourage them to trust that God will take care of it. He is faithful and trustworthy.*

Q: DOES GOD ONLY GIVE US THINGS THAT WE NEED?

69

A: No, he gives us much more. The Bible says that every good thing we have comes from God (James 1:17). That includes all of the things that we need plus all of the extras that he so kindly gives to us. He is able to give us much more than we could possibly hope for or imagine (Ephesians 3:20).

God loves us and he delights in blessing us. Sometimes he lets us have more than what we need—good things that are just for us to enjoy.

Jesus put it this way: "You fathers—if your children ask for a fish, do you give them a snake instead? Or if they ask for an egg, do you give them a scorpion? Of course not! If you sinful people know how to give good gifts to your children, how much more will your heavenly Father give the Holy Spirit to those who ask him." (Luke 11:11-13)

KEY VERSES: *Praise the Lord, I tell myself, and never forget the good things he does for me. He fills my life with good things. My youth is renewed like the eagle's! (Psalm 103:2, 5)*

RELATED VERSES: *Exodus 23:25-26; Malachi 3:10; Ephesians 3:20; James 1:5, 17*

RELATED QUESTIONS: *If what the Bible says about "answering whatever we ask in Jesus' name" is true, why do my parents say he will only answer my need? How come I don't get candy when I pray for it?*

NOTE TO PARENTS: *Encourage your children to talk to God about fun stuff that is important to them, not merely "serious needs." God is interested in your children as they are. They will have plenty of serious topics to talk about soon enough.*

Q: WHY DOESN'T GOD GIVE US SOME THINGS WE PRAY FOR?

70

A: Because God is much wiser than we are. He knows what will happen if we get some of the things that we pray for. He can see all that is happening all over the world in every person's life all the time. He wants the very best for us. He has a plan for our lives and for the lives of every other person. So sometimes God does not give us what we pray for because it might hurt us or turn us the wrong way. At other times God doesn't give us something *right away*. He wants us to wait patiently for his timing. And sometimes God has plans that we cannot understand, so he waits or works something out that we cannot see.

Remember that God will never ignore our prayers. He loves us, hears our prayers, and works things out the best way possible. We can always trust in God's great care for us.

KEY VERSES: *Trust in the Lord with all your heart; do not depend on your own understanding. Seek his will in all you do, and he will direct your paths. (Proverbs 3:5-6)*

RELATED VERSES: *Genesis 21:1-2; Psalms 17:6; 40:1; James 1:6-7; 4:3; 1 Peter 5:7*

RELATED QUESTIONS: *Does God give us the things we want every time? Why doesn't God answer prayer when you ask for a puppy to be there when you wake up? Why doesn't God answer our questions sometimes?*

Q: HOW DO WE KNOW GOD IS ANSWERING OUR PRAYER?

71

A: We know that God is answering our prayers because God said in the Bible that he would. Of course, not all of his answers are yes. Sometimes God answers no. And sometimes he wants us to wait. The answer we receive is not always the one we had in mind, but it is always best.

God is most interested in changing us into his kind of people. That is his main goal for us. Prayer keeps us close to God and helps us understand what he wants us to become. We should pray knowing that God wants to hear from us and that his answer will be best.

KEY VERSE: *I took my troubles to the Lord; I cried out to him, and he answered my prayer. (Psalm 120:1)*

RELATED VERSES: *Psalms 17:6; 40:1; 119:26; 2 Corinthians 12:8-10; James 1:6-7*

RELATED QUESTIONS: *Why doesn't God answer every prayer? What does God say most—yes, no, or wait? When does God answer our prayers? How can we tell if God is telling us yes, no, or wait? Will God tell you yes or no?*

NOTE TO PARENTS: *Children tend to take life as it comes, without connecting events. They may not notice the many answers that God gives to their prayers. Watch for God's answers to your children's prayers. And when you see them, hold a little celebration and thank God together.*

Q: WHY DOESN'T GOD ANSWER PRAYERS RIGHT AWAY?

72

A: God knows more than we know. He has more wisdom than we have. So he gives the answer at the time that is best. Sometimes we do not have to wait at all—God answers our prayers even before we put them into words. At other times we must wait.

God has good reasons for his timing. Sometimes it takes awhile for the answer to come because God is using people and circumstances to answer, bringing them all together like a big team. Or God may know that we are not ready for the thing we want, so he spends a lot of time helping us grow and get ready.

And sometimes God waits to answer in order to test our faith and trust in him. He wants to see if we will keep trusting him even when it looks as if he is not answering. When we decide to keep trusting, our faith becomes stronger, and when the answer finally comes, that helps us trust God even more.

KEY VERSE: *There is a time for everything, a season for every activity under heaven. (Ecclesiastes 3:1)*

RELATED VERSES: *Genesis 21:1-2; 1 Kings 18:42-45; Psalms 40:1; 90:4; Isaiah 55:8-9; Luke 11:5-13; 2 Peter 3:9*

RELATED QUESTIONS: *Will the answer to my prayer be fast? What if we need what we're praying for right away? Do you sometimes get answers to prayer right away? Why does God wait to give you something? Would God answer your prayer quickly if you prayed for someone that was in the hospital?*

NOTE TO PARENTS: *Every child asks this question eventually. Encourage your children through this time to keep on trusting God. Together, ask God to help them keep trusting.*

Q:

IF WE'RE DISCOURAGED AND IT SEEMS LIKE GOD DOESN'T ANSWER OUR PRAYERS, WHAT SHOULD WE DO?

73

A: We should keep on praying. If we are discouraged, we should tell him that we are discouraged. Then we should tell him that we know he is good and has not given up on us.

We should not blame God for our problems or for not answering our prayers. Sometimes bad things happen to test our faith or to make our faith stronger. We should remember that God is teaching us. God will give us strength to keep praying and to keep trusting that he is working things out for good.

Sometimes we are expecting things to work out a certain way. Often God answers in a way we are not expecting. We need to keep looking for his answers.

KEY VERSES: *One day Jesus told his disciples a story to illustrate their need for constant prayer and to show them that they must never give up. Then the Lord said, "Learn a lesson from this evil judge. Even he rendered a just decision in the end, so don't you think God will surely give justice to his chosen people who plead with him day and night? Will he keep putting them off?" (Luke 18:1, 6-7)*

RELATED VERSES: *Luke 11:5-13; Romans 8:28-29; Ephesians 6:18; James 1:2-7*

RELATED QUESTIONS: *Is God trying to teach us something when he doesn't answer right away? Why doesn't God give us what we need right away? How do you know God is talking to you when you pray? Once I prayed for a dog and never got one. Why?*

NOTE TO PARENTS: *When your children are waiting for God to answer their prayers, encourage them by reminding them of times when God has answered past prayers (both theirs and yours).*

Q: WHEN WE PRAY FOR SOMEONE NOT TO DIE AND THEN THEY DIE, DOES THAT MEAN THAT GOD DIDN'T LOVE THEM?

74

A: No, not at all. Every person has to die. That is part of life. When a person dies, it does not mean that God does not love the person or that God does not love the people who wanted that person to live. It also does not mean that someone lacked faith.

The Bible says that God loves *all* people. That is why he sent Jesus to die on the cross. He loved people so much that he sent Jesus to take away the sin of the world.

God hates death, but death is not the end. God's people can look forward to eternal life in heaven with God.

It is OK to cry when our loved ones die. We miss them very much. But if they are Christians, they are going to heaven, and that is much better for them.

KEY VERSE: *The Lord's loved ones are precious to him; it grieves him when they die. (Psalm 116:15)*

RELATED VERSES: *John 3:16; 1 Thessalonians 4:13-18*

RELATED QUESTIONS: *Does God's will always work out for good? Why won't God give you everything you want? How come, when we really pray hard for someone who is sick, they sometimes get worse? Why does God let people die? Does God answer all prayer?*

NOTE TO PARENTS: *Whenever your family prays for someone who is very ill and may die, commit that person to God's care. Ask together that God will do what is best for that person. Ask him also to help friends and family members help and comfort one another.*

Q: IF GOD HAS IT ALL PLANNED, CAN WE REALLY CHANGE IT BY PRAYING FOR THINGS?

75

A: The Bible says that God knows everything, even the future. Nothing takes him by surprise. And he is in control of the world. He rules it all.

Yet we also know that we work with God to accomplish his work. He could do it all without our prayers, but he has chosen not to. Our prayers are part of the way God's work will get done. Prayer is his idea. God wants his people to be coworkers with him in this world, and that means we must pray.

No one can see how their prayers affect God. It is better to pray in faith that God will do what is good than not to pray because we think that it might not make any difference. The main reason for praying is for us to get to know God better and to let him teach and care for us, not just to change things.

KEY VERSE: *The earnest prayer of a righteous person has great power and wonderful results. (James 5:16)*

RELATED VERSES: *Exodus 32:11, 14; Isaiah 55:8-9; Mark 14:36; Romans 8:28-29; James 4:13-17*

RELATED QUESTIONS: *If God knows and can give everything, why can't we have whatever we want? Is God's will different for everyone? What happens if you lose something and pray and it doesn't show up? Why don't I get it when I ask for money? How come God doesn't give you games? How come when we pray for something we want, we only get what we need?*

NOTE TO PARENTS: *Whenever a question like this comes up, remind your children why we pray. We pray to get to know God better and to invite God to change us. That is, we should conform more to God's will, not expect God to conform more to ours.*

ANSWERS TO PRAYERS

WHY DOES GOD NOT ANSWER OUR PRAYERS THE WAY WE WANT?

76

A: God can see into the future, and knows the needs of every person everywhere at all times, so sometimes his answers seem strange to us. He sees what we cannot. Sometimes he answers our prayers exactly as we expect; sometimes the answer is so different that we hardly recognize it.

Sometimes God gives us what we were *really* asking for rather than the specific thing we thought we wanted. Maybe we asked for a toy but really we needed to be happy. God may make us happy *without* the toy, or he may send us a friend to play with instead.

If we trust in God's perfect love, we will always be content with his answers to our prayers.

KEY VERSES: *Dear friends, if our conscience is clear, we can come to God with bold confidence. And we will receive whatever we request because we obey him and do the things that please him. (1 John 3:21-22)*

RELATED VERSES: *Isaiah 55:8-9; Romans 8:28-29; Ephesians 3:20; 1 John 5:14-15*

RELATED QUESTIONS: *Why would God give us something we don't want? How come I always get sweaters and stuff for Christmas when I pray for toys? I have prayed for many things, but God hasn't given them to me. Why? Why doesn't God grant what we want? Because I thought he was supposed to make us happy.*

NOTE TO PARENTS: *Sometimes we are amazed at how God answers our prayers, but other times the answer comes so subtly that we wonder if God really did it or it just happened. Encourage your children with the fact that God is everywhere, knows everything, and is in control. If you prayed about it, God arranged it, subtly or miraculously.*

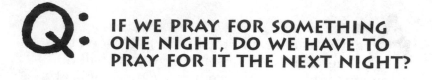

Q: IF WE PRAY FOR SOMETHING ONE NIGHT, DO WE HAVE TO PRAY FOR IT THE NEXT NIGHT?

77

A: We do not have to keep praying the same prayers over and over, but it is good to pray every day for the things that really matter to us. It is all right to keep praying for the same thing when we don't see an answer and when it is important. Also, continuing to pray for the same thing has a way of changing us. While we are praying, God may show us a different direction to take or a new attitude to have. God uses prayer to change us. So it is good to keep praying for what matters to us.

KEY VERSE: *Be glad for all God is planning for you. Be patient in trouble, and always be prayerful. (Romans 12:12)*

RELATED VERSES: *Luke 18:1-8; Acts 1:14; Ephesians 6:18*

RELATED QUESTIONS: *Is it wrong to stop praying when you get tired of praying about the same thing every day? Should you pray for the same thing every time? Why does God not give us something until we've prayed enough? Why do people say prayers again and again? Why would God answer your prayer the fifth time you pray but not the first? If we keep on praying about something, will God answer our prayer? Does God answer prayers that have been said over and over again? Why should we not keep silent until God answers our prayer? Do people have to keep on praying and give God no rest?*

NOTE TO PARENTS: *The Bible tells us what we should pray for regularly (see questions 26–29 and the section "What to Pray For"). Help your children learn and add new kinds of prayers one at a time. Suggest topics (a little different each time) that will help them add to their prayer life slowly and progressively.*

Q: HOW COME GOD ANSWERS SOME PEOPLE'S PRAYERS AND NOT OTHERS?

78

A: God answers the prayers of the people who love him. The Bible says, "The earnest prayer of a righteous person has great power and wonderful results" (James 5:16). This verse teaches that a person who knows God and obeys him prays the kinds of prayers that God answers.

But not everyone in the world is part of God's family. Only people who have put their faith in Jesus are God's children. People who do not know God may pray, but they do not have the assurance that God will act on their request.

In the end, no one knows why God does what he does. God has plans for every person's life, and he works out those plans in his wisdom. We trust that his plans for us are good, and we trust that his plans for others are good too. We should not judge people or pretend to know why God does something for this person but not for that one.

KEY VERSE: *The Lord hates the sacrifice of the wicked, but he delights in the prayers of the upright. (Proverbs 15:8)*

RELATED VERSES: *Psalm 17:1; Luke 18:9-14; Hebrews 5:7; James 5:16*

RELATED QUESTIONS: *Does God answer everybody's prayers? Does God give us things if we're good or bad? Why do people think that God will listen to other people more than them?*

NOTE TO PARENTS: *Children tend to think that God rewards good people with answered prayer and punishes bad people with unanswered prayer. Remind your children that God answers prayers out of his love and grace. He does not use our works to determine who gets this or that blessing.*

Q: WHY DO SOME PEOPLE WRITE DOWN WHEN GOD ANSWERS THEIR PRAYER?

79

A:

Usually people write down God's answers to prayer because they want to remember how God has blessed them. Many passages in the Bible tell about people who did this. These people wrote down what God did for them in the past so that they would not forget and so their children would know about it too.

When we remember what God has done for us, we can thank and praise him. We can also be encouraged to keep praying and to live for him. It helps to go back and read about all the times just like this one when God answered prayers for which we patiently waited, especially if it looks as if God is not answering our prayers now.

KEY VERSE: *Think of the wonderful works he has done, the miracles and the judgments he handed down. (Psalm 105:5)*

RELATED VERSES: *Deuteronomy 6:12; Psalm 63:6*

RELATED QUESTIONS: *If we wrote it in a book every time God answered prayer, would we find that God always answers our prayers at some time or another? Is it wrong to not record it when God answers your prayer? Does God always answer prayer? Will God answer our prayers?*

NOTE TO PARENTS: *You can help your children make a "faith story" book for themselves and record in it the details of God's answering prayer. You might want to do one for the whole family.*

Q: HOW DOES GOD ANSWER OUR PRAYERS?

80

A: God answers our prayers in many ways. God is all-powerful, so he can use anything he wants to work out his plans. One of the ways he answers prayer is by using other people. For example, God often uses doctors and medicines to bring healing. He uses generous Christians to give money to people in need, in answer to their prayers.

God also uses other means. Sometimes he uses angels to do miracles or to intervene in some invisible way. He also uses events and the forces in nature.

Sometimes God simply changes *us*. For example, we may ask for more money, and God may answer by showing us how to use what we have more carefully. In other words, God gives us wisdom and teaches us; he works inside us to make us more like Christ in the way we think, talk, and act.

KEY VERSE: *You faithfully answer our prayers with awesome deeds, O God our savior. You are the hope of everyone on earth, even those who sail on distant seas. (Psalm 65:5)*

RELATED VERSES: *Psalms 81:7; 118:5-21; Daniel 10:12-14; 1 Corinthians 12:6-7; 2 Corinthians 1:11; Philemon 1:22*

RELATED QUESTIONS: *How does God make your prayer requests come true? Will candy fall out of the sky if you pray for it? How can God care for everyone in the world in one day? Why can't we hear God answer? Why doesn't God talk to you when you pray? Why does God answer our prayers?*

NOTE TO PARENTS: *Our children need to know that nothing can stop God from answering their prayers and nothing is too big or too small for him to do. He is always able, and he is always willing to work things out for our good.*

Q: WHEN GOD SAYS WE CAN PRAY ABOUT ANYTHING, DOES HE REALLY MEAN ANYTHING?

81

A: God always means what he says, so indeed we can talk with him about anything at all—feelings, requests, questions, anything we can think of. God invites us to come to him with whatever is on our mind. This does not mean that we will *get* everything we ask for, but we can pray about anything.

Prayer is not magic. It is a talk with God, who is a person. What matters most is that we trust in God and do what he says.

KEY VERSES: *[Jesus said,] "You can ask for anything in my name, and I will do it, because the work of the Son brings glory to the Father. Yes, ask anything in my name, and I will do it!" (John 14:13-14)*

RELATED VERSES: *Matthew 18:19-20; John 16:23-24; Philippians 4:6-7; 1 Peter 5:7*

RELATED QUESTION: *Does God give you anything if you have enough faith?*

82

A: Jesus said that even if we have a very tiny amount of faith, we can accomplish great things in prayer. Having faith just means that we believe that God is faithful. In other words, we decide to trust that he loves us and will do what he said he would do. Great faith in God comes from having a little faith and deciding that God is faithful and that we are going to trust him no matter what.

We should put all our trust in God and depend on him, not on our own words, strength, or clever plans. If we trust even a little in our mighty God, it will make a huge difference.

KEY VERSE: *"You didn't have enough faith," Jesus told them. "I assure you, even if you had faith as small as a mustard seed you could say to this mountain, 'Move from here to there,' and it would move. Nothing would be impossible." (Matthew 17:20)*

RELATED VERSES: *Psalm 22:4-5; Mark 9:22-24; Luke 17:6; James 1:6-7*

RELATED QUESTIONS: *Is there ever enough faith? Why do people think if they have enough faith in God they will get anything? Why do people think that one way or another they can get whatever they want when it is not true?*

NOTE TO PARENTS: *A man wanted Jesus to heal his son. Jesus said, "Anything is possible if a person believes." The man replied, "I do believe, but help me not to doubt!" (Mark 9:23-24). Jesus healed his son. Sometimes we, like that man, doubt God. Whenever this happens with your children, let them know that God loves them and is willing to act on their behalf. Then lead them in asking God to overcome their doubt.*

PRAYING FOR OTHERS

Q: HOW DO WE KNOW WHO TO PRAY FOR?

83

A: We should pray for whomever we care about, and we should also pray for people in need, for pastors and missionaries, for government leaders, and for ourselves. For example, we can pray for family and friends. We can pray for people that we know are having trouble. We can pray for the pastor of our church, for the missionaries that our church supports, and for our Bible teachers. We can pray for our elected leaders, judges, lawmakers, school board superintendents, teachers, and other leaders. We can even make a list and pray for them regularly.

It is always good to pray for ourselves. We can ask God to teach us, to give us wisdom each day, and to make us grow in our faith.

KEY VERSES: *I urge you, first of all, to pray for all people. As you make your requests, plead for God's mercy upon them, and give thanks. Pray this way for kings and all others who are in authority, so that we can live in peace and quietness, in godliness and dignity. (1 Timothy 2:1-2)*

RELATED VERSES: *John 17:1-26; Romans 8:26; Colossians 1:3, 9-12; 1 Thessalonians 5:25; James 5:13-16*

RELATED QUESTIONS: *Can you pray for anyone, anywhere? Do a lot of people always have to pray for one person? Why doesn't God always make miracles?*

Q: HOW DOES PRAYING HELP SICK PEOPLE FEEL BETTER?

84

A: Sometimes God answers our prayers for a sick person by causing the person to get better. Perhaps we pray that the doctors will have wisdom, and God makes them think of a treatment that cures the disease.

Other times God helps the sick person learn to live with the illness. Perhaps the person cannot walk, but God teaches the person how to be joyful with God's love and care instead of walking again. Or the person becomes kind and caring toward others who are suffering because of what he or she has gone through.

One kind of healing makes the person's *body* better, and the other kind makes the *person* better. So praying for sick people is very important.

KEY VERSES: *Are any among you sick? They should call for the elders of the church and have them pray over them, anointing them with oil in the name of the Lord. And their prayer offered in faith will heal the sick, and the Lord will make them well. And anyone who has committed sins will be forgiven. (James 5:14-15)*

RELATED VERSES: *Psalms 103:1-5; 147:3; Isaiah 38:1-8; James 1:2-4*

RELATED QUESTIONS: *If you're sick, is it selfish to pray that you'll get better? Is it bad to not pray for someone who is sick? How can God touch someone? Why do people call the elders to pray for them?*

NOTE TO PARENTS: *Prayer is a natural response to sickness. Encourage your children to pray for people who are sick, but be sure to explain that the outcome is in God's hands.*

Q: HOW COME MISSIONARIES NEED SO MUCH PRAYER?

85

A: Because their work is very important, and they often run into problems that make their work difficult. They are telling people about Jesus. Only God can change people's minds and hearts. So we pray that God will open the hearts of people to the gospel message that the missionaries are telling. It is very important that people hear and understand the message of Jesus.

At the same time, missionary work is very difficult. Satan does not want missionaries to succeed in what they do. He will give the missionaries trouble and problems that make their work frustrating. For example, some people may speak against the missionaries. Or the missionaries may get sick. So we pray that God will keep Satan away from the missionaries and make them strong and able to do their work.

Missionaries depend on our prayers. If we do not pray, they will have a very hard time telling others about Christ.

KEY VERSES: *Don't forget to pray for us, too, that God will give us many opportunities to preach about his secret plan—that Christ is also for you Gentiles. That is why I am here in chains. Pray that I will proclaim this message as clearly as I should. (Colossians 4:3-4)*

RELATED VERSES: *Romans 15:31; Ephesians 6:19-20*

RELATED QUESTIONS: *Why do missionaries need people to pray for them? Why should you pray for missionaries?*

NOTE TO PARENTS: *Try to introduce your children to at least one missionary. The best candidates are missionaries who are relationally close to you or are from your church. Go hear them speak at your church the next time you have opportunity to do so. You can also open your home to missionaries who are on furlough. Kids find it easier to pray for people they know than for strangers.*

Q: WHAT DO PRAYER WARRIORS DO?

86

A: Some people use the term "prayer warriors" to describe people who seem to pray all the time. They pray for others and for God's work on a regular basis. They know that prayer is important. Because they care about God's work in the world, they make sure that they pray about it often.

God wants all of us to pray for others, for Christian leaders, and for the growth of his kingdom. But some people feel that God has given them an extra special task of spending a lot of time doing this.

KEY VERSE: *Timothy, I thank God for you. He is the God I serve with a clear conscience, just as my ancestors did. Night and day I constantly remember you in my prayers. (2 Timothy 1:3)*

RELATED VERSES: *Daniel 6:10; Luke 2:36-37; Acts 6:3-4; 1 Thessalonians 3:10; 5:17*

RELATED QUESTIONS: *What are intercessory prayers? What makes someone a better pray-er? Are prayer warriors and intercessors the same thing? What does "intercessory prayer" mean? What are intercessors, and why do we need them? Who are prayer warriors? Why do some people call themselves prayer warriors?*

PRAYING TOGETHER

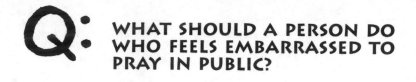

Q: WHAT SHOULD A PERSON DO WHO FEELS EMBARRASSED TO PRAY IN PUBLIC?

87

A: It is OK to pray in public as long as we are not showing off. We should not feel ashamed of it or embarrassed. But some people are shy. When they are asked to pray aloud, they feel very awkward. They are afraid that they will say something wrong and that people will laugh at them.

We must remember that we do not pray to impress others. Whatever we pray is all right if it comes from the heart. So when we are asked to pray in public, we can just talk to God in our own words and in our own way.

KEY VERSE: *Then I will declare the wonder of your name to my brothers and sisters. I will praise you among all your people. (Psalm 22:22)*

RELATED VERSES: *Psalm 96:3; Matthew 6:5-6; Luke 9:26; Romans 1:16*

RELATED QUESTIONS: *What if your friends make fun of you if you pray in church? Do you have to pray if you are asked to pray? Are some people given the gift of being able to speak to God freely in front of others, while others stumble on words?*

NOTE TO PARENTS: *At a certain age, some children will become self-conscious about praying in public. You can teach them to pray in front of others (and help them get used to it) by having them take turns saying the mealtime prayer. Start simple, and expand it to include a current family issue or two.*

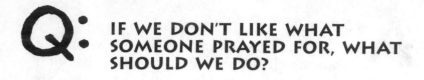

Q: IF WE DON'T LIKE WHAT SOMEONE PRAYED FOR, WHAT SHOULD WE DO?

88

A: Nothing. We should let people lead us in prayer and not judge them or what they say. Some people become used to certain patterns of praying that may seem strange to us. We should be careful not to scorn them just because we do not like their choice of words or style of praying. They may just have a different way of asking God for something. But remember that God cares most about the heart of the people praying, not the specific words they use.

Sometimes we can learn from others' prayers. If we do not like what someone prayed for, we should thank God that the person prayed and then think about what we can learn from the person's prayer. We should always be open to learning new things from others. We should especially be glad that they are praying.

KEY VERSE: *Stop judging others, and you will not be judged. Stop criticizing others, or it will all come back on you. If you forgive others, you will be forgiven. (Luke 6:37)*

RELATED VERSES: *Matthew 7:1-5; Romans 14:10-13*

RELATED QUESTIONS: *Why do you have to pray together in a church? I thought the people made up the church, not the building. Do you have to pray in church? Why do people pray in church?*

Q: WHY DOES GOD WANT US TO PRAY TOGETHER?

PRAYER MEETING IN JASON'S ROOM AT BEDTIME. ALL WELCOME

89

A: God enjoys it when his people pray together because it is one of the ways we can help and support one another. The Bible calls Christians a "body." This means that they work best when they work together, like the different parts of a body. When believers pray together, they strengthen and encourage each other. They complement each other. And they can share prayer requests and pray for each other. It is powerful.

KEY VERSES: *[Jesus said,] "I also tell you this: If two of you agree down here on earth concerning anything you ask, my Father in heaven will do it for you. For where two or three gather together because they are mine, I am there among them." (Matthew 18:19-20)*

RELATED VERSES: *2 Chronicles 7:14; Psalm 34:3*

RELATED QUESTIONS: *Why does God like us to pray with other people? Why do people pray together at church but sometimes not at home? Why do a lot of people pray when there's a real need or someone is sick?*

NOTE TO PARENTS: *Always be ready to pray with your children. When they have a need or you both see a need, pray about it together. Ask your children to pray for you, too, and give them specifics. Also let your children know that you are praying for them.*

DO CHILDREN HAVE TO PRAY WITH AN ADULT?

90

A: Not at all. Jesus said, "Let the children come to me. Don't stop them!" (Luke 18:16). Any believer, no matter how old or young, can talk with God alone. God loves to hear from his children. He welcomes all sincere prayers.

Go ahead and practice praying to God all by yourself. You can start by telling him what is on your mind and asking him to help you solve your problems. You can also ask him to teach you to pray better. You do not have to do it a certain way; it is like talking to your friends— you just tell them what you want to say in your own words. Then thank God for understanding what you want to say, even if you don't know how to say it.

KEY VERSE: *You have taught children and nursing infants to give you praise. (Psalm 8:2)*

RELATED VERSES: *Matthew 6:6; 19:13-15; Luke 18:16; Romans 8:26-27*

RELATED QUESTIONS: *Should you pray alone? Is it OK to pray alone? Is it bad to pray alone all the time? Do you have to pray with anybody? Do you have to pray by yourself? Why do some kids think they have to pray with an adult?*

NOTE TO PARENTS: *When your children start praying on their own, you have successfully primed the pump. But do not leave them there. Continue getting together with them for prayer so that you can continue to help them while also encouraging them to pray on their own. If there is something they want to pray about privately, without your hearing it, don't pry it out of them; encourage it. It shows that they are starting to trust God with private and important concerns. That is very good.*

91

A: It can be. Group prayer can be more powerful than individual prayer because it helps believers grow closer to each other as well as closer to God. It gets a lot of people praying for the same thing. It is also a great way of showing God that we agree about what is important.

Group prayer is one way God helps us. We may not feel like praying, or we may not feel very confident in our prayers. So others pray with us to help us receive God's strength and help. In that way it is more powerful because we can get our prayers answered even when we are feeling weak.

KEY VERSE: *And let us not neglect our meeting together, as some people do, but encourage and warn each other, especially now that the day of his coming back again is drawing near. (Hebrews 10:25)*

RELATED VERSES: *Matthew 18:19-20; Acts 1:14*

RELATED QUESTIONS: *Can we pray by ourselves? What about the people who pray alone? I think it's OK to pray for yourself, and God will listen, but is it better to get more people involved? It's good to have a lot of people, but why do you have to have so-o-o many people to make the prayer more powerful? Is it bad to pray by yourself?*

NOTE TO PARENTS: *A good time to teach your children the importance of group prayer is when your family is going through a tough time. You can call the family together, explain the situation and what you want to tell God, and then pray together.*

Q: WHY DO SOME PEOPLE HOLD HANDS WHILE THEY'RE PRAYING?

92

A: Holding hands with others when we pray can help us feel together and more like we care for each other. Also, holding hands can be a sign that we all agree in what we are talking to God about. People in a family or small group do not have to hold hands when they pray together, but sometimes they like to.

KEY VERSES: *May God, who gives this patience and encouragement, help you live in complete harmony with each other—each with the attitude of Christ Jesus toward the other. Then all of you can join together with one voice, giving praise and glory to God, the Father of our Lord Jesus Christ. (Romans 15:5-6)*

RELATED VERSE: *1 Corinthians 1:10*

RELATED QUESTIONS: *Does holding hands increase the power of prayer? When people pray together and hold hands, isn't that because they are really agreeing? Why do we hold hands and close our eyes when we pray? Does it mean anything to hold hands while we pray?*

NOTE TO PARENTS: *Holding hands when you are praying with your children can help them concentrate and not fidget so much. But also let your children know that holding hands is not essential.*

BEDTIME PRAYERS

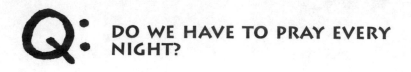

Q: DO WE HAVE TO PRAY EVERY NIGHT?

93

A: No. God has not set exact times when we *must* pray. Prayer is simply something that we should do every day. A lot of people like to pray every night and try to keep that habit because they know that prayer is important, and the end of the day seems to be a good time for them. Others prefer to pray in the morning before they start the day. Some people set aside special time to pray in the middle of the day. Praying at night is a good habit, but it is not a rule that we have to follow. Each of us should pick the time of day that works best for us.

KEY VERSE: *Timothy, I thank God for you. He is the God I serve with a clear conscience, just as my ancestors did. Night and day I constantly remember you in my prayers. (2 Timothy 1:3)*

RELATED VERSES: *Psalms 42:8; 55:17; 119:147-148*

RELATED QUESTIONS: *Why do we pray every night? Do you have to pray at night?*

NOTE TO PARENTS: *As your children get older, they may want to change the time of their devotional prayer. Encourage them to pray during a part of the day when they can concentrate and be consistent.*

Q: WHAT IF GOD HAS ALREADY ANSWERED ALL OF OUR PRAYERS?

94

A: First of all, we can thank him for answering them! We can be glad, tell God thank you, and praise him for being so good to us. Then we can tell someone else about it so they know about the great things God has done for us. And then we should think about new requests we can bring to him. If we cannot think of anything *we* need, we can think of other people who need prayer. We can pray for the people in our family, for our friends, for our leaders, and even for our enemies. Then we can pray for wisdom and that God will teach us new things. There's always something to talk to God about.

KEY VERSES: *Give thanks to the Lord, for he is good! His faithful love endures forever. Has the Lord redeemed you? Then speak out! Tell others he has saved you from your enemies. (Psalm 107:1-2)*

RELATED VERSES: *Psalm 118:21; Philippians 4:4; James 5:13-18*

RELATED QUESTION: *What if we have absolutely no prayer requests or praise reports?*

NOTE TO PARENTS: *Encourage your children to tell God what is on their mind even if they don't have a request to make. As they get older and develop their relationship with God, they will get more comfortable with different kinds of prayer. And when you pray with them, let them hear you talk to God about what is on your mind so that they can see that not all prayer has to involve a list of needs.*

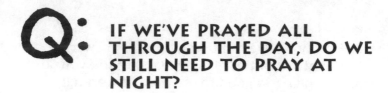

Q: IF WE'VE PRAYED ALL THROUGH THE DAY, DO WE STILL NEED TO PRAY AT NIGHT?

95

A: We should try not to think of prayer as a requirement that we have to meet. Instead, we should make a habit of praying. We should pray about things that matter to us. And we should pray honestly and privately.

Remember that prayer is an opportunity to talk to God, who knows us and loves us. If we know him and love him, we will pray often because we know he is on our side. We will pray simply because we love God. But we will not worry whether we have prayed enough.

Bedtime is a good time to pray because we can think through the day and pray about the next day. But we do not need to think of bedtime prayer as a chore to do. If we have already spoken with God about our concerns, we can just thank him for taking care of us as we drift off to sleep.

KEY VERSE: *Keep on praying. (1 Thessalonians 5:17)*

RELATED VERSES: *Psalm 55:17; Luke 2:37; Ephesians 6:18*

RELATED QUESTIONS: *What would happen if you didn't pray at night? Why do we have to say a prayer before we go to bed? Why do you have to pray at night?*

NOTE TO PARENTS: *Do not force children to pray. Always present prayer as an opportunity to do something good and pleasing to you and to God. This will help your children see prayer as a positive activity that they can do.*

Q: ARE YOUR DAYTIME PRAYERS AS EFFECTIVE AS YOUR NIGHT ONES?

96

A: God does not hear prayers better during the day than during the night. And God does not care what time of day we choose to pray. What God cares about is our attitude. He wants our prayers to be honest and heartfelt—he wants us to say what is on our mind.

Some people find it easier to pray at night than during the day. Perhaps they become more easily distracted during the day, thinking about all the things they have to do and the places they have to go. They may have trouble concentrating on their prayer during the day. For them, praying at night may be better.

Others find it easier to pray during the day because they become drowsy at night. They cannot concentrate on praying at night because they too quickly fall asleep.

It is always good to pray, whether it is nighttime or daytime. God always loves to hear from us.

KEY VERSE: *Night and day we pray earnestly for you, asking God to let us see you again to fill up anything that may still be missing in your faith. (1 Thessalonians 3:10)*

RELATED VERSES: *Mark 1:35; Luke 6:12; 2 Timothy 1:3*

RELATED QUESTION: *Why is there a set time to pray?*

Q: AFTER OUR PARENTS PRAY WITH US, DO WE STILL NEED TO PRAY ON OUR OWN LATER?

97

A: We certainly can. We do not have to pray only with our parents. If we have our own private requests that we want to bring to God, we should go ahead and do so. It is OK to tell God whatever we like. He loves us and cares for us and loves to hear anything and everything we want to say to him, as long as it is respectful.

But we do not have to pray on our own in order for God to love us or to answer our requests. If we happen to pray mostly with our parents, God does not mind. The important thing is that we pray.

KEY VERSES: *Jesus said, "Let the children come to me. Don't stop them! For the Kingdom of Heaven belongs to such as these." And he put his hands on their heads and blessed them before he left. (Matthew 19:14-15)*

RELATED VERSES: *Luke 18:15-17*

RELATED QUESTIONS: *I think praying with parents is good, but what if you have a personal prayer and want to be alone? Why do we have to pray with our parents? Why do parents pray with us on a regular basis instead of just once in a while? Do you have to pray with your mom and dad? Why do parents pray with children?*

NOTE TO PARENTS: *It is great for you to pray with your children; it lets you lead them to God and teach them how to pray. But be sure your children also know that God welcomes their private prayers. If they are afraid of "not saying it right," tell them that God is very happy with the way they pray all by themselves and that he will help them grow. Remind them that Jesus welcomes children.*

Q: WHY ARE WE SOMETIMES FORCED TO PRAY? SHOULDN'T WE PRAY WHEN WE WANT TO?

98

A: Prayer is a good thing to do, just like brushing our teeth, taking a bath, and eating good food. We may not always enjoy praying, but we should do it whether we feel like it or not.

Sometimes parents make children pray even if they don't feel like it or want to. There is nothing wrong with that. If we always waited till we *felt* like eating good food, we would probably eat nothing but cookies and ice cream. Then we would get sick, fat, and weak. We simply need to do what we ought to do. This is true of prayer, too. And prayer is much more important than eating good food, taking a bath, or anything else.

The good news is that God rewards those who discipline themselves to pray. They soon find that they miss it when they cannot do it. God changes us as we pray, and that is just one more reason we should work at it.

KEY VERSE: *Devote yourselves to prayer with an alert mind and a thankful heart. (Colossians 4:2)*

RELATED VERSES: *Colossians 3:17; 1 Thessalonians 5:17-18*

RELATED QUESTIONS: *Why do our parents remind us to pray? Why do parents tell us to pray when we are bad? Why do parents make us pray when we already have? It drives me crazy!*

NOTE TO PARENTS: *Be careful never to use prayer as a punishment. Do not make children pray as penance or as a way of making them think about God. Make prayer something to look forward to. And if they do not want to pray, tell them that's OK, and pray for them aloud as they listen. Lead them; do not push them.*

HOW CAN WE THINK OF SOMETHING GOOD TO PRAY ABOUT IF WE'VE HAD A BAD DAY?

99

A: Even when we have had a terrible day, we have good things to pray about. For example, God is good—we can thank him for being good, for being in control, and for caring about us. We can tell God about our bad day and what makes us upset about it. Then we can ask him to help us with our bad situation. Also, we can express confidence in God's goodness and in his willingness to help us. We can say that we are glad he is with us.

Praying and praising God is a good way to take our mind off our troubles.

KEY VERSE: *No matter what happens, always be thankful, for this is God's will for you who belong to Christ Jesus. (1 Thessalonians 5:18)*

RELATED VERSES: *Psalms 43:1-5; 69:16-18; James 1:2-4*

RELATED QUESTIONS: *Why should you thank God for a good day if you had a bad day? Why do we have to pray even if we are in a bad mood? Is it bad not to pray even if you are in a bad mood? If we have a bad day, will God still forgive us if we don't pray? Why do we thank God when we've had a bad day? Do we have to thank God for the day, or could we ask him for other things instead?*

NOTE TO PARENTS: *It is very reassuring to a child for Mom or Dad to pray for him or her. Whenever your children have a bad day, pray for them. Express sadness at the things that have made your children sad, ask God to help, and express confidence that he will help. This will do more to calm and comfort them than making them pray.*

Q: DO WE HAVE TO PRAY EVEN IF WE'RE TIRED?

100

A: Just before Jesus was arrested, he asked his disciples to stay awake and pray, but they fell asleep. It is difficult to pray when we are tired, but we should not let tiredness keep us from talking with God. We should try hard to make a habit of praying, even if it is sometimes inconvenient.

KEY VERSE: *"Why are you sleeping?" he asked. "Get up and pray. Otherwise temptation will overpower you." (Luke 22:46)*

RELATED VERSES: *Proverbs 6:6-11; Mark 14:37-38; Luke 6:12*

RELATED QUESTIONS: *Will God punish us if we're too tired to pray at night and our parents told us to? Does it matter if you're too tired to pray at night? God already knows everything.*

NOTE TO PARENTS: *If your children are too tired to pray, pray for them and let them go to sleep. Tired children do not learn well. And if your children are often too tired to pray, consider changing your family's bedtime routine so they are more awake at prayer time.*

Q: IS IT BAD TO FALL ASLEEP WHEN WE ARE PRAYING TO GOD?

101

A: No, it is not bad to fall asleep while praying. In fact, there is no better way to fall asleep. If we are in bed and want to talk to God until we fall asleep, that is a wonderful thing to do. It is always good to pray.

But if we are falling asleep because we pray *only* when we are tired, then we need to find another time to pray so we can also pray when we are awake. It is always good to set aside times for prayer when we can think clearly and not get distracted.

KEY VERSE: *Through each day the Lord pours his unfailing love upon me, and through each night I sing his songs, praying to God who gives me life. (Psalm 42:8)*

RELATED VERSES: *Psalms 3:5; 4:8; 63:6; Matthew 26:39-45*

RELATED QUESTIONS: *When people fall asleep when they're praying, does God know what they would have prayed if they had stayed awake? Some people pray, and in the middle of praying they fall asleep. Why? Why do people fall asleep right in the middle of a prayer? Does it really matter if people fall asleep in the middle of their prayers? Because God knows everything! Is God mad when people fall asleep during prayer?*

Q:

HOW COME SOME PEOPLE ARE ASKING FOR SUNSHINE WHILE OTHER PEOPLE ARE ASKING FOR RAIN?

102

A: People ask God for different things because they have different needs and different concerns. A baseball player might ask God for sunshine so she can play her game. At the same time, a farmer nearby might ask God for rain to help his crops to grow. Fortunately, God sees everything and knows what is best. He can work out all things everywhere for everyone's best because he is infinite and all-powerful. We can be thankful that God is wiser than we are and that he sees the whole picture, not just one part of it!

KEY VERSE: *For our God is in the heavens, and he does as he wishes. (Psalm 115:3)*

RELATED VERSES: *2 Samuel 15:25-26; Matthew 5:45; Romans 8:28-29; James 5:17-18*

RELATED QUESTIONS: *Does God just answer the prayer for the weather he wants? Who cares if it rains or shines? I don't; I'm thankful for every day. Shouldn't we just pray for God to give us the weather the land needs? Why do people ask for rain or sunshine? Why do people pray for rain?*

NOTE TO PARENTS: *Do not discourage your children from praying for things like weather just because the answers may not come as asked. Explain that God hears and cares but must consider what is best. Have them pray something like "God, if it is possible, I'd really like sunshine for our camping trip. But I trust you can work things out in another way too. Please work it out in the way that is best."*

Q: CAN WE PRAY FOR SNOW SO WE CAN'T GO TO SCHOOL?

103

A: We can talk with God about anything that is on our mind. But we should not make silly, selfish, or foolish requests. For example, we *could* pray that money would fall from the sky, but that would be both silly and selfish. Praying for school to be called off would be foolish. We should do what is good and wise, and that includes going to school. We should try to match our desires with God's. Instead of treating him like a genie, we should treat him like our loving Father and wise, almighty God.

KEY VERSE: *Take delight in the Lord, and he will give you your heart's desires. (Psalm 37:4)*

RELATED VERSES: *Matthew 6:9-10; Luke 22:41-42*

RELATED QUESTIONS: *Is it wrong to ask God to make it snow? Does it bug God if people always pray about snow or rain? Would God make snow in the summer?*

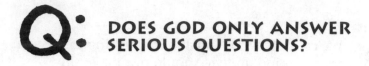

Q: DOES GOD ONLY ANSWER SERIOUS QUESTIONS?

104

A: God cares about us. He does not limit himself only to "major" problems, such as life-threatening illnesses, wars, and natural disasters. God tells us to bring *all* of our concerns to him. If something is important to us, we should talk to him about it. We should not try to guess what God is thinking or what he might approve of.

It is true that God does not want us to pray silly prayers. Prayer is not a joke. But God is always ready and willing to hear our honest concerns, no matter how "small" they may seem to us.

KEY VERSE: *Give all your worries and cares to God, for he cares about what happens to you. (1 Peter 5:7)*

RELATED VERSES: *Psalm 139:1-18; Philippians 4:4-10*

RELATED QUESTIONS: *Why is God so wonderful? Does God just answer the person that he feels like answering?*

NOTE TO PARENTS: *Encourage your children to pray about all of their concerns, no matter how small those concerns may be. If we reserve prayer for "serious" issues, we give the impression that we should pray only to get out of jams. We also make the mistake of assuming we know what is truly serious and what is not. All of our concerns are serious to God.*

Q: IS IT OK TO COMPLAIN TO GOD?

105

A: Yes, it is all right to complain to God. We should be honest about our feelings, and we certainly cannot hide them from God. Anyone who reads the Psalms and the book of Job can see that the people who prayed told God how they really felt. But they also did not accuse God of doing something wrong. They did not accuse him of losing control or of doing something bad. They told God that they believed in his goodness. That is how we should pray too.

We can and should tell God how we feel. Also, we should tell him that we know he is God and has our best interests in mind. We should thank him for loving us.

God is on our side. He will come alongside and help us if we trust him.

KEY VERSES: *How long, O Lord, must I call for help? But you do not listen! "Violence!" I cry, but you do not come to save. Must I forever see this sin and misery all around me? Wherever I look, I see destruction and violence. I am surrounded by people who love to argue and fight. (Habakkuk 1:2-3)*

RELATED VERSES: *Job 3:1-10; Psalms 77:1-20; 102:1-28; Ecclesiastes 7:13-14; Habakkuk 1:1–2:1; 1 Peter 5:7*

RELATED QUESTION: *Why can't we know everything when we're born?*

NOTE TO PARENTS: *There is a difference between complaining to God and lashing out at him in anger. Lead your children to see God as their ally, loving Father, and best friend. Lead them from their complaint to an expression of faith in God and trust in his goodness.*

Q: DOESN'T GOD EVER GET TIRED OF ANSWERING PRAYERS?

106

A: Nope. God never gets even a little bit tired of answering prayers. He loves to hear from us because he loves us. Jesus died for our sins so that we could have friendship with him. That does not change no matter how often we ask things of him.

God wants to work in our lives to change our behavior, thoughts, and habits. We should never fear that we are wearing him out with our prayers, even when we pray the same thing over and over. That is because he wants to keep being a part of our lives.

KEY VERSES: *O Israel, how can you say the Lord does not see your troubles? How can you say God refuses to hear your case? Have you never heard or understood? Don't you know that the Lord is the everlasting God, the Creator of all the earth? He never grows faint or weary. No one can measure the depths of his understanding. (Isaiah 40:27-28)*

RELATED VERSES: *Proverbs 15:8; Hebrews 4:14-16; 10:19-22; 1 Peter 5:7*

Q: WHAT IS THE LORD'S PRAYER?

A: It is a prayer that Jesus gave to his disciples when they asked him to teach them how to pray. Jesus did not call it the Lord's Prayer, but people since then have called it that. It gives a good model for all Christians to follow in their prayers. It tells us what kinds of things God wants us to focus our prayers on.

Take a look at the Lord's Prayer from time to time. It can give you ideas of what to pray for.

KEY VERSES: *Pray like this: Our Father in heaven, may your name be honored. May your Kingdom come soon. May your will be done here on earth, just as it is in heaven. Give us our food for today, and forgive us our sins, just as we have forgiven those who have sinned against us. And don't let us yield to temptation, but deliver us from the evil one. (Matthew 6:9-13)*

RELATED VERSES: *Luke 11:2-4*

RELATED QUESTIONS: *Why aren't there names for all prayers? What does* hallowed *mean? How can a kingdom come?*